MW01258971

"Salary negotiation doesn't
learn, practice, and improve. Read *Fearless Salary Negotiation*,
take notes, then follow Josh Doody's step-by-step negotiation
process. Your future self will thank you."

- **Josh Kaufman**, bestselling author of *The Personal MBA*
and *The First 20 Hours*

Fearless Salary Negotiation

A step-by-step guide to getting paid what you're worth

Josh Doody

Copyright © 2015 Josh Doody

All rights reserved.

ISBN: **0692568689**

ISBN-13: **978-0692568682**

For my family, my greatest source of inspiration and encouragement.

Contents

About the author

Josh Doody dual-majored in Computer and Electrical Engineering, and later earned his MBA at the University of Florida. He began his professional career as an electrical engineer, then transitioned to project management and consulting in the talent management software industry.

He has worked in many areas of the talent management industry including project management, consulting, implementation, technical support, and product development. He has consulted with firms large and small on their compensation management and planning strategies and helped implement software to help them manage their workforces more effectively.

Josh has also been a hiring manager, helping to build a 25-person technical support team based at the headquarters of an international software company, and has managed a team of technical consultants.

Introduction

When I ask people what keeps them from getting paid what they're worth, I hear one word over and over again: *scared*.

"I am *scared* to counteroffer."

"I am *scared* to ask for more money."

"I am *scared* to ask for a better job."

"I am *scared* they will pull my offer if I ask for too much."

Over and over again, I hear how *scared* people are to demand that they are paid what they're worth. Most of their fright is simply a fear of the unknown.

...

In *Indiana Jones and the Last Crusade*, Indy has to get through a series of deadly obstacles to find the chamber where the Holy Grail is held. One of those obstacles is called "the leap of faith" because he is confronted with a seemingly uncrossable chasm. This chasm is terrifying because the only way forward is to cross it, but it's so wide and so deep that it seems that certain death awaits anyone who tries.

Indy realizes that he simply has to make a leap of faith, so he stands at the edge of the precipice, closes his eyes, leans his head back, sticks one leg straight out in front of him, and falls forward into the chasm. And, seemingly miraculously, he doesn't fall to his death and instead seems to float above the chasm a few feet from the ledge.

Then the camera moves around to show us that a bridge, camouflaged to blend in with the walls so that it is invisible from Indy's vantage point, spans the chasm. He carefully moves across the bridge to the other side.

Indy went from being terrified of the seemingly uncrossable chasm to being totally fearless, and the only thing that changed was that he found the bridge that spanned the unknown.

...

Understanding salary negotiations, promotions, and raises is the bridge across the chasm of fear that keeps so many people from taking a leap of faith for themselves.

Fearless Salary Negotiation is a guide to getting paid what you're worth. But it's also something deeper—it's an exposé on how companies determine salaries and job titles, and how they think about raises and promotions. It is my way of showing you how to successfully bridge the chasm between what you think you know about salaries, job titles, and pay structures, and how they actually work.

How to get the most out of this book

There are really two ways to read this book: read it straight through or use it as a reference. Or both, of course. The best way to understand what *Fearless Salary Negotiation* is about is to just read the book straight through. Then you'll have a full picture of how to estimate your market value, how to interview effectively, how to negotiate your salary, how to leave a job on the best possible terms when the time comes, and how to get a promotion or raise.

However, if you need a specific topic *right now*, you should have no trouble jumping right to the relevant chapter and reading through it without any background. And if you're *really* in a pinch—you have an interview tomorrow or you just got an unexpected job offer and need to know what to do next—you could even jump straight to the Summary of the relevant chapter and skim it to get a quick overview. Later on, after you've read the entire book, you can use it as a reference for each specific topic as your career requires it.

Part 1 is about understanding your market value. It includes a quick overview of how companies manage their salary structures and an easy-to-follow method for estimating your market value.

Part 2 is about getting paid what you're worth when changing companies. The key chapter is "How to negotiate your new salary", and the other chapters are extremely important for taking full advantage of that chapter. Acing your interview will help you get the absolute most out of your negotiation. Leaving your job on the best possible terms is a wise thing to do in order to maximize your longevity and future prospects in your industry.

Part 3 is about getting paid what you're worth within your current company. If you like your company and think you're under-paid, then pursuing a promotion or raise may be a great way to increase your pay and stay with a company you enjoy.

...

Fearless Salary Negotiation is one component of a full suite of tools and resources to help you get paid what you're worth. The suite includes the book, case studies, video courses, and other great resources.

A special offer: Learn more about the full suite of tools and resources available for *Fearless Salary Negotiation* at FearlessSalaryNegotiation.com, and *use the offer code* **paperback1** *to get $5 off when you upgrade.*

You can also get the email templates from the book, a salary negotiation worksheet, and other tools for free at FearlessSalaryNegotiation.com/extras.

PART 1

Understanding your market value

A few foundational concepts

This part of the book is very short and will only take a few minutes to read, but it covers some foundational concepts that will give you a clearer lens through which to view the rest of the book. "How companies manage their salary structures" not only gives you a quick survey of commonly used terminology, but also gives you a clear picture of how salaries are managed and determined behind the scenes.

"How to estimate your market value" gives you a three-phase approach to estimating your market value by looking at your industry, your geographic region, and within your own company.

Both chapters will come in handy repeatedly throughout the book, so I encourage you to take a few minutes to read through them and refer back to them later on.

CHAPTER 1

How companies manage their salary structures

This chapter isn't *required* reading, but you should read it anyway. It's tempting to jump right into "How to negotiate your new salary" or "How to get your next promotion", and you can definitely do that. But this is a very quick primer that will help you understand *why* my methods work, and it will give you some context for the next chapter, "How to estimate your market value".

It's short, so give it a quick read!

Overview of paygrades, bell curve, and raises

Before we talk about *how* to get a promotion or raise, we need to talk a little about how companies typically structure pay scales. This is important because it helps explain why all raises aren't created equal. Sometimes, it's really tough to get a 5% pay bump, and sometimes it'll be relatively easy to get a 10% pay bump or greater.

So let's talk about some common terminology and I'll explain how salary structures work while we're at it.

Jobs, job titles, and positions

A *job* is a set of responsibilities to be performed by an employee. That set of responsibilities is usually described in a "job description", which you've probably seen before. Most jobs have a *job title* like "Consultant" or "Accountant" or "Senior Developer".

For any given job, there might be multiple *positions*, which are "seats" available for that job. A company might have five or six Jr. Developers, for example.

Career paths

A career path is a series of jobs in succession. For example, a typical career path for a Software Developer might be something like this:

Jr. Developer → Developer → Sr. Developer → Team Lead → Director of Software Development → VP of Software → SVP of Software → CTO → CEO

Paygrades (or paybands)

Most companies are structured so that each job has a *paygrade* or *payband* that describes the lower and upper ends of the pay range for that particular job. I'll refer to them as "paygrades" from here on out because that's the most common industry term.

Paygrades are usually labeled something pretty generic like "E01" or "F2" or even just "1". Each job (Mechanical Engineer, Accountant I, Operations Manager) maps to a paygrade, and multiple jobs may map onto the same paygrade. For example, "E01" may translate to something like "New Engineer", so "Electrical Engineer I" and "Jr. Software Developer" and "Mechanical Engineer I" may all map to the "E01" paygrade.

A paygrade is usually bounded at the lower and upper ends by a salary. The *bottom* of a paygrade is the minimum salary available to jobs assigned to that paygrade. The *top* of a paygrade is the maximum salary available to jobs assigned to the paygrade. The *midpoint* is the salary at the middle of the paygrade—half way between the bottom and top.

Salary structure

A *salary structure* is a way of describing a series of paygrades. It's essentially a summary of various paygrades and the jobs they represent along with their salaries.

Here's an example of a salary structure to show you what this looks like with a visual:

Name	Bottom	Midpoint	Top	Job
E03 —	$80k [	=====|=====	] $100k —	Sr. Developer
E02 —	$70k [	=====|=====	] $90k —	Developer
E01 —	$60k [	=====|=====	] $80k —	Jr. Developer

So, a Jr. Developer is in a paygrade named "E01" that goes from $60,000 (the bottom of the paygrade) to $80,000 (the top of the paygrade). Then a Developer is in a paygrade called "E02" that goes from $70,000 to $90,000. And a Sr. Developer is in a paygrade called "E03", which goes from $80,000 to $100,000.

The paygrades are often pretty wide and have some overlap so that they look like a set of stairs if you graph them.

That example is totally made up, but is a good representation of a typical set of paygrades for Developers. And note that a Mechanical Engineer I—an entry-level Mechanical Engineer—may *also* be in the E01 paygrade.

Promotions

Promotions happen when you move *up* to the next job in your career path, and it usually represents a jump to a higher paygrade as well. In our example above, this means stepping up to the next paygrade. If you look closely at the example, you'll see that many of the paygrades overlap, which implies that you can be promoted without getting a raise. For example, a Jr. Developer making $75,000 could theoretically be promoted to Developer without a pay increase by moving from the higher end of the "E01" paygrade to the lower end of the "E02" paygrade.

This usually doesn't happen, but that's how it *could* happen.

Raises

Raises are when you move to a higher salary. This may mean just moving "up" (to the right, toward the top of the paygrade) in your current paygrade, or it could mean moving into a higher paygrade *and* moving "up" within that new paygrade.

Counterintuitively, being *lower* in your paygrade is better for your prospects of getting a raise while staying in that paygrade. The higher you are in your paygrade, the less room there is before you bump into the "top" of the paygrade, and that's often a hard limit. Even if a big raise wouldn't bump you into the top of your paygrade, it can still be difficult to get into that top part because the tippy-top of a paygrade is often reserved for people who have been in that paygrade for a long time, and either aren't being promoted or don't *want* to be promoted.

Here's an example to show what I mean.

Let's say you're a software developer and you are hoping for a $10k raise. How easy it will be to get that raise depends very heavily on where you are in your current paygrade. If you're a Jr. Developer making exactly $60k, then a $10k raise would move you to your paygrade's midpoint. That isn't a difficult move because you still have a lot of room to move up in your paygrade without bumping into the upper limit, even after your raise.

On the other hand, let's say you're a Developer and you are hoping for a $10k raise, but you're already at $85k. It's going to be very difficult for you to get that raise because it moves you above the top of your paygrade. The closer to the top of your paygrade you are, the harder it is to increase your salary while remaining in the paygrade.

So, what can you do?

The best thing is to try to get promoted so you move into a higher paygrade with room to breathe at the top. The Junior Developer can make a good case for a $10k raise based on job performance, and will have a good chance of getting that raise without needing a promotion. The Developer's best bet is to pursue a promotion to Senior Developer while pushing for that $10k raise. $95k will still be near the top of the Senior Developer paygrade, but it won't be *above* the top of that paygrade, so it's more feasible.

How do you find out what the paygrades look like?

The short answer is that you probably can't, at least not for your specific company. I've worked at one company that told me the midpoint of my paygrade (but not the bottom and top bounds). Every other company I have worked for has protected their paygrade information like a trade secret.

You could try asking your manager where you are in your paygrade, and it's possible your manager will tell you "the low end" or "the high end" or "near the middle". But you probably won't get much more info beyond that.

Still, there are some things you can do to guesstimate your position in your paygrade.

You may know what some of your colleagues are making, and that will give you a sense of how wide the paygrade actually is. In some places, it's taboo to talk about salary. But sometimes people are more open about this, especially coworkers who have been together for a while in a smaller setting.

Market rates

You can also look at industry pay to get a sense of where you stack up. *Salary.com* and *glassdoor.com* are good places to start. Those sites will give you a sense of what other people with your job title, skillset and experience in your industry or region are getting paid, including a midpoint. That gives you a sense of the answer to this question: "If I left my current job and went to do a similar job at a different company, what could I expect to be paid?"

You might be thinking something like, "But those sites would only give me a sense of where I might be relative to the average paygrade at a bunch of other companies. That doesn't tell me where I am in my paygrade at my current company." That's sort of true. In reality, those sites reflect *market rates* or "market pay" for your skillset, and most companies use market research to determine their own salary structures. They're not just making up paygrades in a vacuum—they're doing research to figure out what people are making to do certain jobs in the industry. So there's a bit of a feedback loop that makes *salary.com* and *glassdoor.com* pretty useful: Companies do research to see what other companies are paying, they adjust their paygrades accordingly, they pay their employees according to those salary structures, those employees report their salaries online and elsewhere, and companies do research to see what people are reporting... on and on.

The type of research that companies do to determine their paygrades is quite similar to what you would do by just going to *salary.com* or *glassdoor.com*, but their research is a little more sophisticated and much more expensive.

Why does this matter?

Throughout this book, I give you step-by-step methods to get paid what you're worth. A lot of those methods are based on this concept of paygrades, and how they map to experience and potential salaries.

My salary negotiation methods (negotiating for a new salary and negotiating a raise to increase your current salary) are designed to do two things: Get you in the highest paygrade possible, and get you the most money possible in that paygrade.

For example, the reason you shouldn't give the first number in a salary negotiation is that you don't know what your potential employer's paygrades look like. But they know what their paygrades look like, and they probably have to offer you something in an appropriate paygrade. You can assume they won't come right out and offer you the top number in that paygrade, so their initial offer will give you a sense of the paygrade's midpoint or low end. That's useful information. Of course, you want to maximize your salary, so your counteroffer is designed to get them to either bump you into the top of the paygrade you're interviewing for, or bump you into a higher paygrade.

But if you name the first number, you're doing so totally blind. You might even give a number below the bottom of the paygrade you're interviewing for, so they may have to give you more than you asked for simply because the bottom of your new paygrade is higher than your request. In that case, you may think you get a generous result when they offer you more than you asked for, but you probably cost yourself a lot of money. Why? Because they're giving you the absolute minimum they can give you to get you into that job within their salary structure.

Summary

The more you know about how salaries are structured, what promotions are and so on, the less mysterious this whole subject will be. Much of the fear people feel when negotiating salaries is really just a fear of the unknown—they don't know what they don't know, and the employers seem to know everything.

You don't *need* to know these things to apply my methods, but it will help demystify the subject so that there's less to be fearful about. And that's what this book is about—helping you to be a *fearless* salary negotiator.

CHAPTER 2

How to estimate your market value

A quick note before we get started: Throughout this chapter, I will use "your job" as a catch-all for your *current* job and your *desired* job.

Here's a useful way to think about market value for your skillset and experience: What salary could you expect if you were to go do your job for another company in your industry and geographic area, or if your company were to rehire you as though you had never worked there? That's the market value of your skillset and experience in your industry.

Estimating your market value is both an art and a science. You start by gathering as many data points as you can to get a sense of how others in your industry are compensated for doing jobs similar to yours. From those data points, you can estimate the average market value for your job in your industry. Then consider how you stack up relative to the average person with your skillset and experience to determine the market value for *your* particular combination of skills and experience in your industry.

In short, you'll find a broad average salary for your job in your industry. Then you adjust that average to compensate for *your* particular skillset and experience.

Determining the market value for your skillset and experience

Before you go too much further, you might want to get the market value estimation worksheet that accompanies this chapter at FearlessSalaryNegotiation.com/extras. It will help you keep track of the data you will gather and aggregate throughout the estimation process.

I recommend three primary ways of determining your market value. Some of these may yield more useful information than others. Your goal is simply to gather as much information as you can to estimate your market value.

1. Online research

Spend some time online looking at comparable jobs and salaries in your geographic region.

Market value for the average person

Search online for "[your job title] salary" and spend some time with the first few results, which are usually salary calculators and aggregators. I recommend *salary.com* and *glassdoor.com* as good places to start, but the specific sites aren't important since they could change over time. Some sites are geared toward specific industries, so you may get better data by focusing on sites that cater to your industry if there are any.

What are you looking for? Most sites will usually show a distribution-style description of salaries for a job. They'll have a range—low to high—and they'll identify the midpoint of that range. The midpoint is a good approximation of what the average person doing your job in your industry is paid.

The more data points you can gather, the better sense of the average you'll get. You'll find that these sites might vary quite a bit, so you'll need to use some discretion when determining which ones are more accurate for your industry. Many of these sites also have a job description to go along with the salary estimates, so you may want to give more weight to the salary estimates for jobs whose descriptions look more like your actual job.

How you compare

Then you should consider whether you're "average" or if you're above or below average for your job in your industry. Maybe you have more experience than the average person, or you have a complimentary skill that allows you to contribute more in your job than someone who doesn't have that skill. For example, you may work in marketing for a clothing company, but you also have a background in fashion design. Those complementary skillsets may set you apart from your peers in marketing. If you bring more skills and experience to the table than the average person who does your job, you may be able to pursue a salary above the midpoint you found with your research.

2. Inter-company research

This is tougher to get than the publicly-available salary data online, and easier to get than your intra-company peers' salaries (which we'll cover in the next section).

Market value for the average person

If you know people doing your job for other companies in your industry, you could talk to them to get a sense of what they're paid. Some people are pretty open about this, and there's less of a taboo around discussing inter-company salaries than intra-company salaries.

Some people are uncomfortable discussing *their* salary at all, but there's a nice workaround that you can try: Rather than talking about *their* salary, talk about a salary for a hypothetical person who is very similar to them. For example, you could say, "If someone were hired at your company today to do a job similar to yours, what sort of salary do you think they could make?"

This is an extremely transparent and roundabout way of asking about their salary, but it gives them an out so that they can talk about salaries without explicitly mentioning their salary *per se*.

Note that I suggest finding comparable salaries for your job *in your industry*. This is a subtle but important point—different industries operate with different pay structures and different margins and all sorts of other differences. They also value skillsets differently, and that's a key distinction you need to account for. Finding out that someone with your skillset and experience is paid significantly more in a different industry is good to know because it might mean you should consider looking for work in that industry, but it doesn't necessarily mean that companies in *your* industry will pay the other industries' salaries.

How you compare

Determining how you compare to someone doing your job for a different company in your industry can be tricky because you can't simply observe them doing the job. So you'll need to ask them about it. "What does your day-to-day look like? How many projects do you work on at a given time? Do you do anything in addition to what's written in your job description?"

Then, think about how you stack up. Is your work better than theirs? Worse? Are you faster than they are? Slower? Do you do more things than they do? Fewer?

3. Intra-company research

I don't recommend *asking* your peers for this information, but you may already know it or be able to infer it from water cooler conversations.

Market value for the average person

Most companies (especially in the United States) frown upon openly discussing salaries. This is partly why: if you know what your peers—people doing your job, at your company, in your geographic region—are making, then you have a pretty good sense of what *you* should be making too.

There's not much to say in terms of *how* to figure out what the average person doing your job for your company is making—you either know or you don't. You may be able to discern others' salaries just from paying attention to water cooler conversations, or you may be able to estimate what they're making if you know, for example, that they came into the company at the same time you did, making the same salary you did. People will often talk openly about their merit increase amounts, so you might be able to estimate what they're making now based on your knowledge of their starting salary and what sort of merit increases they've gotten since then.

How you compare

It should be pretty easy to determine how you compare to the average person doing your job for your company. You might work directly with many of those peers, so you can observe them doing the job. As objectively as possible, think about how you stack up. Is your work better than theirs? Worse? Are you faster than they are? Slower? Do you do more things than they do? Fewer?

This is *very* subjective, so you'll need to work hard to be honest with yourself. But this is a good chance for you to understand how you stack up against your peers.

Note that I'm not advocating all-out competition with your peers at your company. You *are* competing for resources (money) with them and everyone else in your company, but you still want to cultivate a positive working environment. You're not looking for opportunities to go head-to-head with your peers—you're just trying to understand how the value you add to the company compares to theirs so that you can estimate how high a salary you can shoot for when negotiating your salary.

Estimating your market value

Now you should have up to three different sets of data on average salaries for your job in your industry—general market data, inter-company data, and intra-company data. You can use these data sets to get a sense of how you compare to the average person doing your job within your industry and your company.

Interpreting the data you've gathered

This step requires you to be as objective as possible. Start with the midpoint for the average person doing your job in your industry. Next, you need to consider all of the data you gathered and get a sense of *your* value relative to the average person doing your job in your industry. Adjust the midpoint value up or down to reflect your specific skills and experience with respect to how much more or less value you bring to the table than the average person's skills and experience.

That's your estimated market value.

Let's look at an example to tie this all together.

An example

Alison is a Project Manager making $65,000 a year in the construction industry. She also has her Project Management Professional (PMP) certification, and she studied Building Construction as an undergrad.

She does some research online and finds that the salary range for Project Managers in Construction in her geographic region is $60,000–$100,000 with a midpoint of $80,000. She is pretty far below the midpoint for the industry. She also notes that most of the job descriptions for Project Managers in the construction industry mention "PMP Certification" as a good certification to have, but it's not a requirement for most jobs.

She knows several Project Managers for other construction firms in her area because she has met them at conferences and trade shows. She has talked to several of those project managers and it seems like they're making around $75,000 and that their jobs are comparable to hers. She also gets the sense that they're as competent and valuable as she is, although most of them don't have a PMP certification. Some of them do have a background in Building Construction, though.

Alison has been working for her company for three years and doesn't know much about what the other project managers are making. She does happen to know that a project manager who left earlier this year was making $73,000, which is a bit more than Alison is making now. She also has a sense that she does better work than many of her peers at her company. People seem to like working with her more, and she's had a few nice awards and some recognition in the past year or so (she hasn't noticed her peers getting as many awards or as much recognition as she has).

So, it seems that the industry midpoint salary is around $80,000 but that those around her are closer to $75,000. She's probably a little better than average, but not much. **Her market value is probably around $80,000, give or take.**

Yes, the "give or take" is really subjective. Given what we know about Alison, $80,000 seems about right, but there's a lot we don't know here. Has her industry been doing well over the past few years? Are project managers in high demand in her industry? Have project managers at her company been let go recently? Those types of things can slide her estimated market value up or down a bit.

If the industry is doing very well, and Alison happens to know that there's high demand for Project Managers, her market value could be $85,000 or even more. If the industry has had a rough few years and Project Managers have been getting let go across the industry, her market value might be closer to $75,000 or even less.

But that's about 25% above her current pay!

It's true, that's a pretty big difference between her current salary and her market value. If her research and analysis were accurate and objective, then Alison is significantly underpaid in her job. If her analysis and research were *not* accurate and objective, then she has manufactured a number that does not represent her skillset and experience in her industry.

It's very important that you do your research and analysis objectively, without a desired dollar amount in mind. Notice that Alison's baseline is based on the industry midpoint, not some arbitrary number that she pulled out of the air. The industry midpoint gives her a frame of reference for the following question: "If I left my company and had to be replaced, or if another company in my industry were to hire someone just like me, what would the company have to pay?" The answer, based on the research Alison has done, is "about $80,000".

Summary

There are three primary methods for gathering data to estimate your market value:

1. **Online research**—Spend some time online looking at comparable jobs and salaries in your geographic region.
2. **Inter-company research**—This is tougher to get than the publicly-available salary data online, and easier to get than your intra-company peers' salaries.

3. **Intra-company research**—I don't recommend asking your peers for this information, but you may already know it or be able to infer it from water cooler conversations.

For each method, you should start by finding the midpoint of the range of market values you find, and then do your best to objectively consider how you stack up against the average. If you are more valuable to your industry than the average person, then your market value is probably above the midpoint; if you are less valuable to your industry—you're less experienced or productive— then your market value is probably below the midpoint.

———————— PART 2 ————————

Getting paid what you're worth when changing companies

Leveraging your best opportunity to significantly increase your salary

The most reliable way to significantly increase your salary is to change companies. The catch is that you only get so many opportunities to take advantage of this fact because most people will only work for a handful of companies during their careers. You have to make these opportunities count.

In Part 2, we're going to focus on maximizing your salary at a new company. There are several interrelated areas where a good plan can really pay off with a successful salary negotiation. Your market value estimation from Part 1 comes into play because it's important to understand your market value so that you can set a realistic goal for your salary negotiation. And you can set yourself up for a successful negotiation by standing out during the interview process and continuously, subtly making your case that you would be a valuable addition to this company.

Getting a strong recommendation from a manager at your new company can also go a long way toward helping you maximize your salary during a negotiation. Many industries seem very large, but you'll find that you keep seeing familiar faces the longer you're in your industry. Those people that you see over and over again could help you find lucrative opportunities, and they may go to bat for you if they see you're interviewing for a job at their company. Those same people could also begin to notice if you're changing companies every couple of years to pursue higher salaries, so make sure you're selective with which opportunities you pursue. You don't want to get a reputation as a job-hopper or it may become difficult to find good opportunities.

You might be tempted to jump straight to "How to negotiate your new salary", but I recommend starting with "How to ace your next interview" and working your way through all of Part 2. The chapters build on each other so that you'll be able to take full advantage of the negotiation chapter if you've already read the interview chapter. Individually, each chapter is useful, but together they can be very valuable because they will give you an overall strategy and the tactics to help you maximize the rare opportunities you will have to significantly increase your salary when changing companies.

CHAPTER 3

How to ace your next interview

Your résumé is out there, your LinkedIn profile is updated, and now you're just hoping some of your applications will turn into interviews. Maybe you've had your eye on one job you *really* want, and they've finally called you to start the recruiting process.

Now what?

The interview is two opportunities in one. It's an opportunity to pitch yourself and convince a company to hire you. And it's an opportunity for you to determine whether you *really* want to do a particular job for a particular company.

There are four phases to the interview process, and if you're a good fit you may repeat the last two phases several times with a given company:

4. Preparation
5. Pre-interview
6. Interview
7. Post-interview

Here's what you need to do in each one of these phases to ace your next interview.

1. Preparation

When an opportunity is on the way, you'll usually get some kind of heads-up: a message on LinkedIn, an email, a voicemail, or even a text message from a recruiter or hiring manager. Once you get the heads-up, you need to do some prep work before you're ready to talk.

Basic company research

Start by spending some time on the company's website, learning about what they do and looking at advertised job openings and job descriptions. Read their blog. Google them to see if there are any recent press releases or articles about them. Check them out on social media.

What do you need to know? You need to know what the company does to make money, who their customers are, how big they are, where they're located, basic information like that. If you were to bump into this company at a dinner party and chat for about 10 minutes, this is the stuff you would learn.

You may have just thought, "Duh. Of *course* I would check out their site," and that's a good sign for you. But you would be surprised how rarely job candidates actually do this, and how much of an impression it can make on an interviewer.

Know which job you're applying for

Read the job description a few times to make sure you get it well enough to answer some basic questions about it and, more importantly, to *ask* some basic questions about it.

Look into other jobs the company is trying to fill

You also need to have a sense of what *other* sorts of jobs they're trying to fill. You can get a good sense of where the company is focused by looking at their "Jobs" or "Careers" page. Are they hiring a lot of sales reps? Engineers? HR folks? Consultants? Managers? If you see any trends like this, take a minute to think about what that tells you about the company itself. Don't read too much into this, but you may be able to identify a need the company has so that you can position yourself in a way that could help the company address that need.

Here's an example:

You notice the company is hiring a lot of sales reps in the western half of the country. That could mean a number of things, but it probably means they're trying to expand geographically and looking to increase top-line revenue. They want to get more customers out west.

Think about how your skillset can help a company like that. If your skillset lends itself well to sales and revenue growth, then you can play that up. If your skillset is in an unrelated area, think about how you can contribute in a way that takes pressure off the company in your area of expertise so they can focus on growing. "I can help you grow" can be just as valuable as "I can help make this other part of the business more autonomous so you can continue focusing more resources on growth."

While you're at it, take note of any other jobs you might be good for, just in case this one doesn't work out. That way you'll have some backup opportunities in mind if you need them.

Prepare for the dreaded salary question

Finally, you need to be prepared to answer the following two-part question:

"So where are you right now in terms of salary, and what are you looking for if you make this move?"

Just so I don't bury the lead: It's best if you *do not* disclose either your current salary or your desired salary during the interview process.

Why you shouldn't reveal your current or desired salary

Once you've completed the interview process, the company will assess your skillset and experience, and determine a range of salaries they're willing to pay you. The range of salaries goes from "If we could get him on board for this salary, that would be a great deal for us!" up to "This is the absolute most we can pay him to do this job."

Your objective with your salary negotiation is to get them as close as possible to the maximum they're willing to pay. You will do this by giving them as many reasons as possible to pay you more *and* by avoiding giving them any reasons to pay you less.

Sharing either your current salary or your desired salary could possibly give them a reason to pay you less (if either or both of those numbers is below the maximum they're willing to pay) and is very unlikely to give them reason to pay you more. So, disclosing either your current or desired salary is risky because it will most likely work against you and could cost you money.

How to respond to the dreaded salary question

If you shouldn't disclose your current or desired salary, then how *should* you respond to the dreaded salary question?

For the "current salary" part of the question, I recommend something like, "I'm not really comfortable sharing that information. I would prefer to focus on the value I can add to this company and not what I'm paid at my current job."

It's true that they may do some digging and put together a good educated guess as to what you're making anyway, but maybe they won't. If they don't know what you're currently making, that makes it more difficult for them to base an offer on your current salary, and that's probably going to mean a higher initial offer for you. It also means that their eventual offer will need to reflect both your market value and the value you'll add to the company without being biased by what you currently make.

The exception is if your current salary is high relative to the market value for your skillset and experience in your industry. In that case, it may help you to tell them what you're currently making to send a signal that you are highly valued at your current company, and that means they will need to work hard to persuade you to join their team by making a very strong offer. But when in doubt, don't share your current salary.

My pat answer to the "what are you looking for" part of the dreaded salary question is, "I want this move to be a big step forward for me in terms of both responsibility and compensation." This answer demonstrates that you want to contribute to the company by taking on additional responsibilities and that you want to be paid well for those contributions.

If they continue to press, even after you give them the answer above, you can say something like, "I don't have a specific number in mind, and you know better than I do what value my skillset and experience could bring to your company."

Here is my recommendation for a good answer to the full dreaded salary question:

"I'm not comfortable sharing my current salary. I would prefer to focus on the value I can add to this company rather than what I'm paid at my current job. I don't have a specific number in mind for a desired salary, and you know better than I do what value my skillset and experience could bring to your company. I want this move to be a big step forward for me in terms of both responsibility and compensation."

Now you're prepared to ace the pre-interview.

2. Pre-interview

Depending on the size and structure of the company you're applying to, the pre-interview may actually be part of the interview itself. I've separated the two concepts (pre-interview and interview) because you'll often have a pre-interview with a recruiter and the actual interview(s) with team members or the hiring manager. But sometimes you'll just jump straight to talking with team members or the hiring manager; in that case, this section will apply to the interview directly.

The recruiter's purpose for the pre-interview is to confirm that you're a good candidate for the job and for the company and subsequently whether they will recommend you for a formal interview. Make sure to build rapport with the recruiter because they're probably your gatekeeper. If they don't like you, they may just drop you from the list of candidates and move on to the next one. They could also be your advocate as the interview process moves forward, and they may even find other opportunities for you at the company if it turns out you're not a good fit for the specific job you've applied for.

The pre-interview is also an opportunity for you to vet the company and the opportunity. Listen carefully and ask good questions so you can decide if you want to continue investing time in the interview process with this particular company.

As for the content of the pre-interview, you've already prepared for this in the preparation step!

Here are some questions the recruiter may ask you during the pre-interview:

- How did you find out about us?
- Why are you interested in working with us?
- How do you see yourself contributing to our company?
- What do you like to do?
- So where are you at now in terms of salary, and what are you looking for if you make this move?

Listen carefully to the questions and give honest answers. Also, try to frame your answers so they apply to this specific company (this won't be a problem because you've already read up on them before this conversation).

Most of the time, you'll also have an opportunity to *ask* questions. This is your chance to figure out if you like the company's mission and vibe, so just ask questions you want answered.

You may learn a lot by asking the recruiter some of these things:

- How long have you been with the company and what is it like working there?
- What can you tell me about the team or group that I would be working with if I get the job?
- What's the company culture like?
- I noticed this trend in your current job openings—what does that say about the company's direction right now?
- Can you tell me about career growth opportunities for this job? What would a long-term career look like at this company?

The "career growth" question may be a good way to learn about the company's salary structure (see the chapter on "How companies manage their salary structures" for more on this topic). If people tend to stay in the role for a long time then the job may be in a wide paygrade, and you might be able to push for a higher salary during the negotiation process. If people only stay in the role for a year or two—true for many entry-level jobs—then the paygrade is probably narrower, and there may be less wiggle room when setting your salary.

Asking about career growth opportunities also shows that you are thinking about a long-term relationship with the company, and that may make them more interested in bringing you on board.

As you're wrapping up, be sure to ask about next steps and how you'll be contacted about them. That way, you can keep an eye on your inbox and spam folder, or you can be ready for their call.

Finally, you might want to ask if you should do anything specific to prepare for a formal interview if you move on to that stage. Most of the time, there won't be anything, but occasionally you'll find out there's a short written skills test or something that you should mentally prepare for.

If the pre-interview went well, and if you still want to pursue the job, your next step will usually be the interview. Here's how to ace the interview phase.

3. Interview

For the most part, an interview is just a conversation between someone who's trying to fill a job (the interviewer), and someone who wants to fill that job (you, in this case). I'm going to call your interviewer "Andy" because this section feels weird if I keep saying "your interviewer" over and over.

We'll start with a general overview of what to be ready for in your interview, and then I'll talk a little about the different venues where you might interview.

Be early

Make sure you show up early so that you're waiting on Andy to begin. Never keep your interviewer waiting—there are few faster ways to make a very bad first impression. Odds are that Andy has just left a meeting, or ended a client call, or scarfed down his lunch so he could make sure you get started on time. If you're late, he'll be frustrated right out of the gate. Frustrated people aren't likely to recommend their frustrators for jobs.

Before the interview begins, make sure you know your interviewer's name if at all possible. (It's "Andy", remember?)

Bring a notebook and your résumé

What this means when you're interviewing in person

Take a notebook and a pen. Don't make a big show of it, but take some notes during your conversation. You may want those notes later, and it looks more professional. (Yes, this is basically just acting. You should still do it.)

Make sure to bring multiple copies of your résumé, printed on good paper with good ink. Assume Andy doesn't already have your résumé, and have it ready if he needs it. You're already bringing a notebook, so put your résumé in there as well.

What this means when you're interviewing virtually

You should have a notebook even if you're interviewing virtually (on the phone or videoconference). This could be a virtual notebook (like Evernote), but you need to be prepared to take notes and let Andy know when you're writing things down.

Have your résumé ready to send electronically if you need to. You've probably already submitted it online to start the application process, so just make sure you have that version of your résumé handy in case Andy doesn't have it.

Introductions

Most of the time, the interview will begin with a little small talk. "So, you know Tom Smith huh?" or "I see you went to Florida State. I'm a Gator, so hopefully we'll get through this okay." Try to give accurate, concise responses. Don't spend 20 minutes talking about that one time Tom jumped off the hotel balcony into the pool at a sales conference a few years ago. Make sure your answers are genuine, and take the opportunity to relax a little bit so that you're both comfortable during your interview.

The question and answer portion

Once things are rolling, there are many different topics that may be covered during your interview. Every interview is different. Even Andy's interviews may vary from day to day depending on his mood, the particular job he's trying to fill, or whether he's bored and feels like doing something different that day.

Make sure to listen carefully to each question, and then consider your answer before you give it. Don't be afraid to ask for some time to think about a particular question before you answer. Sometimes Andy will ask you a question you didn't anticipate, and you'll be caught off guard. It's okay to say, "Wow, that's a good question. I'm just going to think about this for a few seconds before I answer." Then gather yourself, compose your answer in your head, and deliver your answer to Andy. Most interviewers will appreciate that you took the time to really think about your answer rather than just blurting something out. You can do this two or three times in a single interview, but no more than that.

Let's talk about several potential topics you may encounter in your interview so you have a sense of what to expect and how to shine in each situation.

Questions about your résumé

You should know your résumé cold before you start the interview. Make sure you know which previous jobs you've listed, any skills you've listed, accomplishments, all of it. And be ready to talk about everything on there.

Many interview questions begin with, "I see on your résumé that..." This is because it's the easiest place for Andy to go for material, and that may be all he knows about you before he meets you. It's even possible he hasn't seen your résumé before the interview, so he'll likely be scanning it to get a quick sense of who you are as you're introducing yourself.

If you have things on your résumé that you can't talk about (a tool you used for a class project in college, but don't really remember anything about), you should strongly consider taking it off your résumé or noting that you have "basic knowledge of..." that thing. It's not a good sign if Andy asks you specifically about something you have on your résumé and you hesitate and say, "Well, that was a long time ago. I haven't used that in forever."

Questions about you personally

These are often questions about hobbies, side projects, or activities listed on your résumé. Many hiring managers want to be sure you're a good fit for their company and for their team in particular. A good way to figure that out is to learn more about you and, more importantly, to hear you talk about yourself. How you answer questions, your demeanor, how thoughtful or nonchalant you are—all these things give a manager a sense of what it would be like to work with you.

Just relax and answer these questions honestly.

Questions about tools and technology

Andy might ask you about some tools or technology that are in the job description, or that you have listed on your résumé, so be ready to talk about them. Most of the time, you can anticipate these questions by carefully reviewing the job description—there's often a section near the end that lists required and desired skills. Many of those skills will be technology-specific ("proficient with such and such technology").

If it's on your résumé, it's fair game, so make sure you only list technologies you *actually* have experience with.

Technical questions

Andy may ask you technical questions related to the job itself. You can't do too much to prepare for these unless you happen to know they're coming. Just be sure to carefully consider the question and either give your best answer or tell Andy you don't know. This might be a good opportunity to ask for some time to gather your thoughts.

Most of the time, you're being asked these questions because your résumé or something you said indicates that you should know the answer. If you have multiple interviews where you're asked similar technical questions that you can't answer, you may need to study up on that topic so you're more prepared next time. In the meantime, consider revising your résumé to avoid similar questions until you're able to answer them.

Questions about your career goals and aspirations

Be ready to talk about these because they're probably coming. A common one is, "Where do you see yourself in five years?" Yes, it's cliché, but it's also a useful question because it will give Andy a sense of how you're thinking about the job. The best way to give a good answer to this question is to think about it ahead of time.

Specifically, think about it in the context of the company you're applying to.

Frame your answers so that they define how you'll contribute to the company and team you're applying to. A good structure for an answer to this type of question is, "I would like to learn more about [something] and apply that new knowledge to help improve or grow [some business function] within the company. I would also like to help [the team you're interviewing for] be more proficient at [something else]."

"Why do you want to work here?"

Some companies will just come right out with it, so you should be prepared to answer this question. Fortunately, you've spent time reviewing their website and looking at their job openings, so you know what they do and how you can contribute.

Mention things you like about the company in general, and then talk specifically about how your skillset would be a good fit for the company's mission. This is also a good opportunity to mention some good things you might have heard about the company from friends or acquaintances.

Questions about "a challenging situation"

A common one is, "Tell me about a difficult work situation you've encountered, and tell me how you resolved it."

Interviewers ask this type of question because it can provide some insight into how you think about difficult problems in tough situations. You should have at least one of these stories ready to go.

Questions about special projects or side projects you've done

Andy might ask you about special projects you've worked on or side projects you've done on your own time. Make sure you're ready to talk about at least one of these in detail. Before the interview, think about your previous special projects in the context of the company you're interviewing with so that your answer resonates with Andy.

Don't be caught off guard by curveball questions

Interviewers will occasionally throw you a curveball. Sometimes they do this because they want to see how you react when presented with an uncomfortable situation. Sometimes they're just bored.

I've done this myself, and there's usually a method to my madness.

One of my most interesting jobs was building a technical support team from scratch. I was hired specifically to help build a local team, and our goal was to grow the team to 25 people as quickly as possible.

The economy was still in rough shape and our company was in a college town. This led to a unique dynamic: We had far more candidates than we could possibly hire, and all of them had strong technical backgrounds (recent engineering and computer science grads, some Masters grads, and the occasional PhD).

I interviewed several people a week and quickly found that I couldn't use their résumés as any sort of real tool because all the candidates were so technically savvy. So I focused almost exclusively on interviewing for "fit"—I wanted to know how they would work with me, with customers, and with our team. This meant asking questions without caring about the content of the answer so much as its formulation and delivery.

One day, I happened to be interviewing in a very small conference room where the candidates couldn't see anything except me and the wall behind me. It was really, really tight. A candidate came in and sat down, and we talked about his background for a few minutes.

Then I threw him a curveball:

"We're in a pretty small office that has a drop ceiling so there are a bunch of tiles and a few lights above our heads right now. Without looking up, can you estimate how many tiles are in the ceiling?"

I didn't care what answer he gave (I had no idea how many tiles were up there). I wanted to see *how* he formulated his answer to a curveball question. This mattered because customers call into Technical Support with questions just like this all the time. "I logged into the site and it didn't work. Can you fix it?" "What do you mean 'didn't work'? What happened?" "It isn't there." "What isn't there? What did you expect to see? Can you tell me exactly what you did to get there? What did you click?"

In this case, the candidate immediately looked up at the ceiling, then back down at me and gave an answer. He hadn't listened closely and ignored the only constraint I gave him ("don't look up"). Not a good sign. We didn't hire him, and moved on to the next candidate on our list.

I know this seems harsh, but tech support calls are a lot like an interview in that tiny little room—customers will tell you all kinds of useless details, but they won't let you see the ceiling and they demand a solution quickly. It may seem like I asked him this question because I *wanted* him to fail, but I really needed to know if he *would* fail in a similar situation with a customer. I didn't hire him because I didn't want to put him in a situation where he might fail in his job. If I had hired him and he had failed, that would've been my fault.

So how do you figure out how many tiles are up there?

There's no one true way to get the answer, but it's important to listen carefully, acknowledge the constraints, and formulate a plan. It can also help to talk aloud as you think through tricky problems. If you feel comfortable with your interviewer, turn his question into a sort of one-sided discussion so that he can hear you work through the problem. This will give him a good sense of how you think. If you're not comfortable talking aloud while you think through the problem, just tell him you need a moment to think it over.

The wrap-up

Things will usually start winding down when there are a few minutes left. You'll feel the tone shift a little bit from more formal to more friendly. It may feel like the interview is already over, but it's not! There may still be a few great opportunities to make a good impression on Andy.

If you're lucky, Andy will open the door for you by asking whether *you* have any questions for *him*. As a matter of fact, you do!

You can accomplish a couple of things here. First, you can learn more about the company and how this role contributes to it. But you can also leave a good impression on Andy by demonstrating that you were paying attention during your interview, and you came prepared.

You don't want to ask too many questions—two or three is about right. And make sure you're aware of the time—you may have to skip this part if you're already at the end of the allotted time for the interview.

You might want to start with this question: "What does a typical day look like for this role?" Pay close attention to the answer to this question because you could learn a lot that will help you determine whether you really want this job. This is also an opportunity for you to demonstrate genuine interest in the job itself.

Another good question is "What are the greatest challenges for your team right now?" or "What is the greatest challenge for this particular role?"

Both of these questions show that you're already thinking about the job itself and the answers will help you evaluate whether the job is a good fit for you. It's possible you'll hear about the day-to-day and think, "Oh, that sounds terrible." Or you'll hear about the challenges and realize you wouldn't function well in that kind of environment. You're not asking these questions just to sound like you care—you're asking them so that you can evaluate whether you want to continue pursuing the job.

Sometimes, you will have already addressed these two questions organically during the interview. That's okay because we've already discussed some questions you might ask a recruiter in the pre-interview section, and those questions are good here too.

If Andy gives you an opportunity to ask questions, take it. But if you really don't have any questions, don't just ask something to fill the time. It's okay to say, "Well, I was going to ask about the day-to-day work, and about challenges your team faces, but we've already talked about those, so I'm all set!" Andy would rather have 10 minutes back than have to answer silly questions that you're obviously asking just to fill the time, so don't do that.

Venue-specific recommendations

There are a few common venues for interviews these days. The main ones are:

- Telephone
- In-person
- Virtual (Skype video or Google Hangouts)

Almost everything I said above applies to all three venues, but there are a few unique things to consider for each one.

Telephone

Andy will be the one to call you most of the time, so "be early" means having your phone ringer turned on, and being ready to answer the call at least five minutes before the interview is scheduled to begin. If you're calling the interviewer, avoid being early and just shoot for "on time"—you don't want to interrupt Andy's previous meeting if he's in one.

You should also consider wearing headphones so that you can put your phone down to free up your hands to take notes or do discrete Googling. If you pause to take notes, tell Andy that's what you're doing so he doesn't think you've fallen asleep. "I'm quickly jotting that down."

If Andy calls you, you'll have his phone number. Don't use it unless he specifically tells you to give him a call. Just forget you have the number. It's generally okay to send a follow-up email to someone who interviews you, but calling them is a little too personal.

In-person

Your appearance matters because it indicates how serious you are about the job. So put a little effort into looking nice, even if you know the company is very casual.

See if you can find out the dress code for the company and dress one notch above it. If you can't find out on your own (from their website or someone you know who works there), ask the recruiter what the company dress code is. If they're casual, you'll dress business casual. If they're business casual, you'll dress business appropriate.

Virtual (Skype video or Google Hangouts)

Treat this like an in-person interview with respect to your appearance. Make sure to set yourself up at a desk or table rather than sitting on your couch with your laptop. (Yes, I've interviewed people who were just slumped on their couch with their laptop open. No, I didn't offer them a job.)

When you take notes, make sure to give Andy a heads-up so he doesn't think you're just looking down at Facebook on your phone.

4. Post-interview

Now you've aced the Interview, but your work isn't done yet—you still have a few more opportunities to stand out in the post-interview.

First, if you happen to have Andy's email address, shoot him a very, very short email thanking him for his time. You'll also want to discretely share your contact information just in case he needs it later. Unless there's something specific he expects you to follow up on, don't ask any new questions or give Andy any action items in this email. This is just a short email to say "Thanks!" and demonstrate professionalism; it shouldn't require a response.

Here's an example. You can also find this example at FearlessSalaryNegotiation.com/extras.

To: Andy Smith <andy.smith@example.com>
Subject: Josh Doody interview—Thanks for your time!

Hi Andy

I just wanted to say thanks for your time today. It was great to learn more about ACME Corp, and about the Associate Accountant role in particular. ACME Corp sounds like a great company to work for!

Feel free to email or call anytime if you have any follow-up questions.

Thanks again for your time and have a great day!

Josh Doody
josh@example.com
555-555-1234

You'll also want to send an email to the recruiter if that person and Andy are different people. There's one wrinkle here: If you *don't* have Andy's contact information, you'll want to ask the recruiter to thank him for you let him know that you appreciated his time.

Here's an example. You can also find this example at FearlessSalaryNegotiation.com/extras.

To: Shawn Jones <shawn.jones@example.com>
Subject: Josh Doody interview—Thanks for your time!

Hi Shawn

Thanks so much for arranging my interview with Andy today. It was great to learn more about ACME Corp, and about the Associate Accountant role in particular. ACME Corp sounds like a great company to work for!

If you talk with him, please thank Andy for me and let him know I appreciated his time today.

If you need anything else from me, please let me know. Otherwise, I look forward to the next steps in our process!

All the best

Josh Doody
josh@example.com
555-555-1234

How long should you wait to follow up again?

Some companies will let you know if they decide not to move forward with you, and some companies won't. It's difficult to know which you're dealing with, so you may want to send one more follow-up email after about a week to make sure they haven't forgotten about you.

Here's an example. You can also find this example at FearlessSalaryNegotiation.com/extras.

To: Shawn Jones <shawn.jones@example.com>
Subject: Josh Doody interview—Follow-up and next steps

Hi Shawn

It's been about a week since I talked with Andy, so I wanted to follow up to see if you need anything else from me. I'm also curious if you can give me a sense of our next steps in the process.

Thanks for your time and I hope all is well!

Josh Doody
josh@example.com
555-555-1234

Hopefully, Shawn will reach out and let you know they're ready to schedule your next interview. In that case, you're right back to the "Interview" step, and you'll rinse and repeat that step along with the "Post-interview" step until you either get an offer or they let you know, explicitly or implicitly, that they're not going to move forward with you.

We'll talk about what to do once you get an offer in the next chapter, "How to negotiate your new salary".

Summary

The interview is two opportunities in one. It's an opportunity to pitch yourself and convince a company to hire you, and it's an opportunity for you to determine whether you *really* want to do a particular job for a particular company.

Interviews can be intimidating, but they are also relatively predictable. Most interview processes have four phases— Preparation, Pre-interview, Interview, and Post-interview—and if you prepare for all four phases, you will ace the interview process. You'll know you're doing well when you find yourself repeating the Interview and Post-interview phases multiple times with a company.

I recommend reading through this summary section before each of your interviews, just to make sure you're fully prepared. After each interview, take a few minutes to evaluate it and see if you can do anything differently the next time around.

You'll get better with practice, but this should be enough to help you ace your next interview.

1. Preparation

Do basic company research. You should understand the basics of the company—what they do, how they make money, how big they are.

Know which job you're applying for. Read the description a few times to make sure you understand it well.

Know which *other* jobs the company is trying to fill. You can learn a lot about a company by looking at their job openings. See if you can get a sense of where they're currently focused and how you can contribute to helping them get there. Take note of other jobs you might be a good fit for, just in case.

Prepare for the dreaded salary question. They'll probably ask you something like, "What are you making now, and what would you like to make if you get the job?" My recommendation is that you do not give them either number.

Here's a good answer that covers both parts of the question without giving them a number, while emphasizing that you believe you can be a valuable asset to the company:

"I'm not comfortable sharing my current salary. I would prefer to focus on the value I can add to this company and not what I'm paid at my current job. I don't have a specific number in mind for a desired salary, and you know better than I do what value my skillset and experience could bring to your company. I want this move to be a big step forward for me in terms of both responsibility and compensation."

2. Pre-interview

The Pre-interview is usually a separate meeting, but will occasionally be part of the Interview itself.

Build rapport with the recruiter. The recruiter may be your advocate both during the process and later if you're interested in other opportunities at the company.

Be ready to answer questions about yourself and why you want to work for the company. You should already be prepared thanks to your research from the Preparation phase.

Have a few questions ready in case you have an opportunity to ask them. This is a good chance to learn about the company, demonstrate your interest, and continue building rapport with the recruiter.

Before you end the conversation, ask what the next steps will be and find out whether you need to do anything to prepare for the Interview.

3. Interview

Be early. Don't keep your interviewer waiting—that's a horrible way to make a first impression.

Bring a notebook and your résumé. Take notes. It's possible your interviewer won't already have your résumé, so be prepared.

Try to relax and be honest during introductions. It's okay to make small talk for a few minutes so that you and your interviewer can get settled in, but don't spend too much time on this.

Come prepared for different types of questions. Here's a partial list of common types of questions you may be asked:

- Questions about your résumé
- Questions about you personally
- Questions about tools and technology
- Technical questions
- Questions about your career goals and aspirations
- "Why do you want to work here?"
- Questions about "a challenging situation"
- Questions about special projects or side projects you've done

Don't be afraid to ask for some time to think about your answers. This shows "intentionality" and may help you formulate better answers to tricky questions. But don't do this more than a few times during an interview.

Don't be caught off guard by curveball questions. If your interviewer asks you something wacky, just gather your thoughts, listen carefully, and formulate the best answer you can. Make sure to account for any constraints that are part of the question.

When things start wrapping up, look for opportunities to ask questions to learn more about the company and the role you're interviewing for. Here are some good questions you can ask if they haven't been addressed already:

- "What does a typical day look like for this role?"
- "What are the greatest challenges for your team right now?"
- "What is the greatest challenge for this particular role?"

If those questions have already been covered, see if any of your Pre-interview questions might work.

Only ask questions if you can learn new information from them. If you've already covered everything in your interview, it's okay to say, "I think we actually covered everything already!"

4. Post-interview

Email the interviewer to thank them for their time. This email should be *very* brief and should not ask anything of the interviewer.

Email the recruiter to thank them for arranging the interview. If you don't have the interviewer's contact information, you can ask the recruiter to pass along your regards and thank the interviewer for their time. You should also ask the recruiter what the next steps in your interview process will be.

If you haven't heard anything from the recruiter after a week, follow up with one more email. It's okay to follow up with an email a week after your last interview if you haven't heard anything and don't know what the next steps are. Beyond a week, it's likely the company has decided not to continue the process and they just didn't reach out to let you know.

—————— CHAPTER 4 ——————

How to negotiate your new salary

You've aced your interview and the company is about to make you an offer. This is when many people will breathe a sigh of relief and begin to celebrate, assuming the hard work is over. Maybe you're just happy to be leaving your old job, or excited to have a chance to work at a new company.

Don't relax yet! This is an opportunity to make the most of this transition and maximize your salary.

The theory behind my strategy

There are two factors that cause most people to leave money on the table when they negotiate their new salary—lack of information, and reticence to negotiate with a potential employer or manager. This chapter addresses both of these issues.

Reducing information asymmetry

From the moment you start the negotiation, there's a maximum salary the company can or will pay you for your skillset and experience in their industry. Your goal is to get as close to that maximum salary as possible. First, you'll do research to understand your market value and consider the minimum salary you require to accept the job. Then you'll negotiate to maximize your salary.

Squashing that reticence

Here's the headline: You should absolutely negotiate your salary!

Most people don't get many job offers, and they see them as special snowflakes that come along only a few times in a lifetime. This reverence for new jobs spills over into the negotiation process, so they treat negotiations very gingerly, afraid to jeopardize them.

From the recruiter's perspective, your job offer is not a special snowflake. The job you're applying for is probably one of many that particular recruiter is trying to fill, and one of many more that particular company is trying to fill—it's no big deal to them. Most recruiters make job offers *all the time*, and they tend to see everything as numbers—the candidate has an applicant ID, the job requisition has a number, the paygrade for the job is just a range of numbers. If they can get a good candidate at a good salary, that's a good day for them.

It's not just numbers to you because the outcome of this negotiation will affect your life. The numbers have real meaning to you, so you have *far* more skin in the game than the recruiter. But you're leaving money on the table—possibly the equivalent of multiple paychecks per year—if you simply accept the company's first offer and it's in your best interest to negotiate.

I'm going to show you how to approach this negotiation like the recruiter or hiring manager you're negotiating with. Don't be tentative or hesitant. Don't be afraid of offending anyone. Be your own advocate. Fight for as much money as you can get because this is your final chance to maximize your pay *before* you're in the door, confined by the rules for raises and promotions inside the company.

Focus on base salary

We will focus almost exclusively on base salary because your initial base salary has a big impact on your future earning potential. It is the one number that will directly affect every paycheck you get.

Recruiters and hiring managers like to present an offer in terms of "your total compensation package" or "total comp" because that number is usually quite a bit bigger than the base salary. It often includes target bonuses, stock options, etc. I recommend ignoring target bonuses or stock options when you negotiate your salary because the real value of those things is often unknowable. You could hit that bonus, but maybe you won't. Maybe the company will go public, and maybe it won't. Those things are often based on factors totally out of your control that may not come to fruition for many years (if at all), so you can't count on them.

Your base salary is more dependable. And your *initial* base salary affects your salary every year going forward, so that's where you should focus during the negotiation.

In some jobs commission comes into play, but I won't address that directly. Commission is different, and the amount of commission available to a worker varies by industry and job. So I think it's best to just treat commission like a second component of salary and negotiate them together.

The general phases of salary negotiation with a new company

Just like the interview process, the salary negotiation process generally looks very similar across companies.

Here's what the process usually looks like:

1. Preparation
2. Post-interview follow-up
3. Initial offer
4. Your counter
5. Preparing for the final discussion
6. Final discussion

The preparation phase is a solo phase where you will do some research, consider what you want to get from the negotiation, and think about your approach to it. The other four phases may be a series of conversations spread over a number of days, or they could all happen during a single conversation. That's why the preparation phase is so important.

A quick note: I'll be using "counter" as shorthand for "counteroffer" throughout this chapter because it's just easier to use and say "counter". Plus, trust me, you would eventually get really tired of reading "counteroffer" over and over.

1. Preparation

You have two main objectives before you begin negotiating:

1. Understand why you are a valuable candidate for this job
2. Determine the minimum salary you require to do this job

1. Why are you a valuable candidate for this job?

This is extremely subjective, but you've spent enough time researching and discussing this particular job that you should be able to identify what your most valuable attributes are as they relate to the job and the company. Think about them and then write them down.

Start by thinking about what needs this company hopes to meet by filling this particular job. Identifying their needs is key because you can tailor your own pitch to specifically address those needs. The research you did in the preparation phase of your interview process will come in handy as you prepare to negotiate your new salary.

Here are some needs the company may be trying to satisfy:

- They are growing and need help
- They need a specific skillset that they are currently lacking in
- They need more bandwidth—more hands to help distribute the work
- They recently lost expertise or had a position vacated that they need filled to continue operations

Once you have identified the company's needs, you should think about your particular positive attributes that could help address those needs.

Each person and each job is unique, but here are some things you might write down:

- **Applicable experience**—maybe you have prior work experience that will make it easy for you to contribute quickly, with little training or ramp-up time.
- **Availability**—if you can start immediately and contribute quickly, this may help the company if they're in a pinch and need someone now.
- **Coachable and trainable**—if you pick things up quickly, it may help the company to know that you can contribute soon after you start.

Finally, put these together so you can relate your positive attributes to specific needs the company has. Here are a couple examples of some attribute-for-need combinations:

- "You're building a team of salespeople and solution architects to grow into the medical manufacturing vertical, and I have five years of sales experience in that vertical. I can help you grow more efficiently and focus on the right things from the beginning."
- "You're transitioning your application to an Ember front-end, and I've been using Ember for client projects for two years. I can save your team a lot of time because I can come in and start writing code right away."

Notice that a lot of *urgency* is built into these attribute-for-need combinations. This is because most companies see recruiting and hiring as a big expense. A large portion of that expense is new-hire training and onboarding—it takes a lot of time and money to train new people to become productive. You're letting them know that you're valuable because you have this particular skillset *and* you can contribute right away and minimize the onboarding and training expenses required for you to be productive.

We'll come back to this information throughout the negotiation and leverage it whenever there's an opportunity to bolster your case.

2. What is the minimum salary you require to do this job?

Before you go too much further, you might want to get the salary negotiation worksheet at FearlessSalaryNegotiation.com/extras. It will help you keep track of your answers to the questions below, and will help you plan your salary negotiation.

You've probably heard that the key to negotiating is being willing to walk away. Your minimum salary requirement is how you pre-decide when you're willing to walk away from this salary negotiation. This is also the single most important number you'll use when negotiating your salary, and it's your minimum metric for measuring success.

Here are several things you should consider as you determine the absolute minimum salary you'll accept to do this job:

- Your current salary
- Your market value for this job
- The amount you think you can get
- What people in your target job at your target company are currently making
- How badly do they need you? (0–10)
- How badly do you need this job? (0–10)
- When is your next merit increase at your current job?
- When is your next bonus at your current job?

The nice thing about this list is that there's value in just thinking about each item. I recommend that you write down your responses, but if you're not up for that, you should at least take a little time to think about each item. Something may occur to you that will help you find some little bit of leverage you may have otherwise missed.

Let's take each of these items one by one to understand its significance and how it helps you determine your minimum acceptable salary.

Your current salary

Chances are your goal is to increase your salary by taking a new job, so this is your starting point. Plus, it's what you'll ultimately measure your results against when your negotiation is finished.

As I mentioned in "How to ace your next interview", you should *not* share this with the company! This number is for your eyes only!

Your market value for this job

Estimating the market range and your market value for the job you're pursuing is very important. This is your first step in determining the minimum salary you'll accept for this job. Before you can set that minimum salary threshold, you need to understand what your skillset and experience are worth in your particular industry and for this particular job.

This is important for *all* salary negotiations, including raises, so I wrote an entire chapter on the topic of estimating your market value. If you have not already read it, I strongly recommend you save your spot in this chapter and read the chapter on "How to estimate your market value" before you continue.

The amount you think you can get

This is a ballpark number that you'll keep private. It's one metric for measuring your success in this negotiation. It represents what you think you'll get without using what you learn in this chapter. Think of it like this: This ballpark figure is what you'd answer if someone surprised you right after you sent your first application to the company by asking, "If they offered this job to you right now, what do you think they'd pay you?"

My goal in this chapter is to help you exceed this number.

What people in your target job at your target company are currently making

This step is similar to some of the steps in "How to estimate your market value", but it's slightly different. Rather than trying to learn about salaries in your own company or elsewhere in the industry, you're specifically focused on people doing your target job at your target company.

There are a couple ways you could find this out. If you know a manager at this company, they may be able to give you a sense of what your target job pays there.

If you know someone doing your target job at this company, talk to them and see if they can give you a sense what the job pays. You may not want to come right out and ask what they're making, but you can ask a hypothetical question like, "If someone were hired at your company today to do a job similar to yours, what sort of salary do you think they would make?"

It also helps if you can get a sense of how well the person does the job, and how long they've been doing it so that you know how you stack up against them. Then you can get a sense of how your salary might compare to theirs if you were to do the same job they do.

CAUTION: If you are able to find this information, you will *not* explicitly mention it during your negotiation! Pretend you have top-secret intel on the company, and that you're using that intel to your advantage.

How badly do they need you? (0–10)

During your interviews, you may have gotten a sense of how badly they need you or someone else to fill this particular role. This is extremely subjective, but it helps to have a good idea of how badly they need you.

0 means they don't need you at all. Maybe they're interviewing you as a favor to someone who works at the company, and the job wasn't even open.

10 means they're desperate to fill the position as soon as possible and you're the perfect candidate. Maybe they called and said, "Are you available? Frank just left without giving notice and we have to get someone as soon as possible. You're perfect for this role, so we called you first."

Here are some things you can consider to get a sense of how badly they need you: Did they call you, or did you call them? Have they mentioned anything about someone else recently leaving this job? Have they been trying to fill the job for a while? Are they filling one position in this job, or are they filling several positions in this job?

If you find that this number is close to 10, you'll want to tactfully emphasize this during your negotiation.

How badly do you need this job? (0–10)

This one is less subjective.

0 means you could take it or leave it. Maybe you are interviewing as a favor to someone.

10 means you're unemployed, your savings is depleted, and you need a job immediately or you won't make the rent this month. Or maybe you just really, really want this particular job.

If your number is close to 0, you'll want to tactfully emphasize this during your negotiation.

When is your next merit increase at your current job?

This one is pretty straightforward. The point matters to you because you'll want to account for it when considering the minimum salary you need to entice you to take this job. If you're due for a 3% merit raise next month, your minimum acceptable salary might be slightly higher when you account for your pending raise.

When is your next bonus at your current job?

Many companies give semi-annual or even quarterly bonuses, so this is a separate issue from your next merit increase. You may want to account for this when determining your minimum acceptable salary, and it could also come in handy in the final stages of your negotiation when you consider non-salary benefits. For example, you may use your upcoming bonus as justification for requesting a signing bonus:

"I'm due for a bonus next month, and my on-target bonus for this quarter is $2,000. It's really going to sting to miss out on that. Can we talk about a signing bonus to help offset that loss?"

A few more things to consider before setting your minimum acceptable salary

In addition to all the things we discussed above, there are a few more things you might consider when deciding the minimum salary you will accept to do this job:

- **How do you feel about your target company?** The better you feel about the company, its culture, your potential co-workers, etc., the more this might push your minimum acceptable salary to a lower number.
- **How do you feel about your target job?** The more excited you are for this particular job and the opportunities it affords you personally and professionally, the more this might push your minimum acceptable salary to a lower number.
- **Are there perks that make this particular opportunity more attractive?** For example, maybe it would reduce your commute by 30 minutes a day, or you would get to work with technology that you're more comfortable with. The more appealing the perks, the more this might push your minimum salary to a lower number.

Picking a number: The absolute minimum salary you will accept before walking away from the opportunity

It is important that you determine your minimum acceptable salary now, when you are objective and clear-headed, as opposed to waiting until you're in the midst of a negotiation when things can get fuzzy. Deciding now may keep you from making a spur-of-the-moment decision (accepting less pay than you require) if you get involved in a stressful negotiation. More importantly, making this decision in advance gives you some leverage in your negotiation—if the recruiter or hiring manager senses that you're serious about walking away, they will be more careful to make you an offer in your acceptable range (even if they don't know exactly what that is).

This is an extremely subjective personal decision. You're really trying to answer the following question: "What is the minimum salary I need to leave my current situation and take this job?" You're hoping to make *more* than this number, but you would be happy making this salary, and you will not accept the job for a base salary less than this number.

Now is the time to decide: **What is the minimum salary you will accept to do this job?**

Think about this long and hard because it really matters. When you set this number, you should stick to it unless you discover significant new information that forces you to change it.

Got your number? Then you're ready to negotiate your new salary.

2. Post-interview follow-up

Once you've finished interviewing, you'll usually hear from the recruiter or hiring manager, asking if you're free to chat about your interview process and next steps. This will usually be a pretty short conversation—10 minutes or so. They just want to make sure you're still interested in the position, and they're almost always going to take one last shot at getting you to disclose your desired salary.

This is your final opportunity *before they make you an offer* to make the case that you should get as much money as possible. Odds are the company has a *range* of salaries in mind that they may offer you, but they haven't yet decided on the specific salary they will offer. By making a good case for yourself in the post-interview follow-up, you may be able to push their offer to the higher end of the range they have in mind.

You have two objectives for your post-interview follow-up call:

1. Don't give the first number in your salary negotiation.
2. Make your final case that you will be a valuable asset to the company and that they should make as strong an offer as possible.

1. Don't give the first number

The recruiter's last attempt to elicit your desired salary will probably sound like this:

"Okay, I just need to talk to Finance and your hiring manager to see whether we're ready to move forward with an offer. What sort of salary did you have in mind for this job? I just want to have something to run by Finance. And do you have any questions for me before we move forward?"

If you read the chapter on "How to ace your next interview", you may recognize the second part of "the dreaded salary question" in the recruiter's dialogue above.

Here's the dreaded salary question again, to refresh your memory:

"So where are you right now in terms of salary, and what are you looking for if you make this move?"

Maybe you got away without disclosing a desired salary the first time, but now you feel more pressure to play ball because you're so close to an offer. Don't give in! Instead, give an answer something like this:

"You know, I really don't have a specific number in mind right now. I've learned a lot through the interview process, and I look forward to hearing what you suggest so I can consider it. As I mentioned earlier in this process, I want this move to be a big step forward for me in terms of both responsibility and compensation..."

2. Making your final case

Notice that I ended the answer with an ellipsis this time? That's because the *next* thing you'll say is:

"...because I know I can immediately contribute to help you address [this need] with [this positive attribute], and [this other need] with [this other positive attribute]."

Turn the dreaded salary question redux into an opportunity to make a case for yourself just before the recruiter goes to Finance to determine the salary they'll offer you. This is why you spent time doing research and thinking about the company's needs during the preparation phase of your interview process (see "How to ace your next interview" for more on this) and again during your preparation for this negotiation. Now you can identify specific attribute-for-need combinations to describe how you will address specific needs and add value to the company.

The recruiter may cover other things too, but it's a successful call for you as long as you meet your two objectives. The call will usually end with the recruiter saying they just need to reach out to Finance and your hiring manager to see if the company will move forward with an offer, and they'll let you know when they're ready to move forward.

The next thing you hear from them will likely be your initial offer.

3. Initial offer

The initial offer may arrive in a few forms, ranging from informal to formal. Many companies prefer to make the initial offer verbally. The recruiter or the hiring manager will reach out and ask if you have some time to chat, then set up a call where they'll deliver the offer at a high level: base salary, bonus structure, any stock options, and maybe a possible start date. Sometimes the initial offer will come in an email.

Regardless of how they deliver the initial offer, you should answer something like this:

"Thank you so much for the offer. I would like to take a day or two to think it over before I respond."

That's the straightforward version, but you can beef it up with something like, "...I just want to run it by my spouse to make sure we're on the same page," or "...I just need to talk it over with my family before I respond."

In general, the more time you have to think it over and determine your counter, the better. Shoot for a day or two, and it may help if you can stretch it over a weekend.

You may also want to ask some questions about the offer, but keep in mind that you are not negotiating yet. You might ask about start date, or ask for clarification on benefits, or confirm how many vacation days you would get, but you're not countering or accepting yet. Not even if you really like the offer! Okay?

4. Your counter

They've finally made you an offer, and *they* threw out the first number because you didn't give in to the dreaded salary question. Now what? You need to determine your counter.

This is an important step because you will almost certainly be leaving money on the table if you don't counter. It's very unlikely that the company offered you the maximum amount they're willing to pay because they usually leave some room to negotiate in case you do counter.

I've made this strategy as straightforward as possible so that it is easy to follow, even when you're under pressure.

"But what if I really like the offer?"

You could just accept it, but I don't recommend that because if they immediately made you an offer you really like, there's a pretty good chance you underestimated your market value in the preparation phase of this process. You should re-evaluate your answers to the questions in the preparation section of this chapter, focusing on your market value, how badly they need you, and how badly you need this job.

In fact, now is a good time to go back and look at those answers to refresh your memory before we jump into the numbers. Go ahead, take a few minutes to review your answers in the preparation section, then come back here and we'll figure out your counter.

Ready?

Determining your aggression factor

Before we can calculate your counter, we need to determine how aggressive you can be.

Remember those two "0–10" questions we looked at during the preparation phase? We're finally going to use them!

We're going to do some very light math here. Here's the formula for your aggression factor:

[How badly they need you] - [How badly you need this job]
= Your aggression factor

Here's a quick example: Let's say you are pretty sure the company needs you to do this job pretty badly, but you don't need this particular job too badly. "How badly they need you" would be about an 8, and "How badly you need this job" would be about a 3. That means the formula would be 8 - 3 = 5. In this situation, your aggression factor is 5.

If your aggression factor works out to be less than zero, just set it to 0. That means your aggression factor should always be a number between 0 and 10.

Pretty easy! Make sure you keep this number handy because we'll come back to it in a little bit.

Okay, now we're ready to determine your counter.

Determining your counter

By waiting for them to make the first offer, you learned more about the range of salaries they're willing to pay and gave yourself an opportunity to formulate a counter based on their offer so that you can get as close as possible to the *maximum* they're willing to pay.

So how do you determine your counter? There are two scenarios we need to address. The most common scenario is when they offer at least your minimum acceptable salary. The other scenario is when they offer less than your minimum acceptable salary.

Let's start with the more common scenario.

1. When they offer at least your minimum acceptable salary

Most of the time, they'll offer something at or above your minimum acceptable salary. This makes sense because your minimum acceptable salary is a conservative number you chose that represents the minimum it would take to get you in the job, whereas their offer is designed to be high enough to entice you to take the job while leaving them some wiggle room to negotiate if you counter.

Since you've already got your minimum acceptable salary locked up, you can turn your focus to maximizing your salary before your tenure at the company begins. The first step to maximizing your salary is to make a counter that pushes the company higher into the range of salaries that they're willing to pay you while not pushing too hard. So how do you do that?

A good range for a counter is between 10% and 20% above their initial offer. On the low end, 10% is enough to make a counter worthwhile, but not enough to cause anyone any heartburn. On the high end, 20% is a pretty big difference between their offer and your counter, but it's not so big that it will come across as excessive when used in the right situation.

We need to determine where in the typical counter range— between 10% and 20%—you should counter. This is where your aggression factor comes into play. You just add your aggression factor to 10% and that's how much you should counter above their offer. In our example above, your aggression factor was 5, so your counter would be 15% above their initial offer (10% plus 5% for your aggression factor).

Let's look at an example. Say your minimum acceptable salary is $50,000 and the company offered you $55,000. They met your minimum, so now you just need to determine an appropriate counter. Your aggression factor is a 5, which means your counter should be 15% above their offer. In this case, 15% of $55,000 is $8,250, which means your counter should be $63,250. It can be a little easier to work with round numbers, so you might round to $63,500.

2. When they offer less than your minimum acceptable salary

Your goal for the negotiation has now shifted from "maximize my salary before I start this job" to "try to get my minimum acceptable salary or more if possible". It's frustrating, but this is why you prepared by choosing your minimum acceptable salary in advance—you know the salary you must get to in order to take the job.

You have two main options in this situation. The most obvious option is to simply tell the recruiter or hiring manager that you can't accept less than your minimum acceptable salary and see if they'll agree to that salary. This is the most direct route, but it has the downside that it caps your possible salary at your minimum acceptable salary. So before you do that, let's see if there's still a way to get *more than* your minimum acceptable salary.

The real question is whether you can reasonably counter a high enough salary that a negotiation will lead to a salary greater than your minimum acceptable salary. Here's our rule of thumb: Use the method in the previous section to determine what your counter would be. If that number is greater than your minimum acceptable salary, then that is your counter. If that number is less than or equal to your minimum acceptable salary, then just tell the recruiter or hiring manager that you can't accept less than your minimum acceptable salary.

Let's look at two examples to illustrate this point. For both examples, let's say your minimum acceptable salary is $50,000 and your aggression factor is 5. That means your counter will be 15% above their offer unless their offer is so low that your counter isn't at least $50,000.

Scenario 1—When your counter exceeds your minimum acceptable salary: Let's say they offer you $45,000. Fifteen percent of $45,000 is $6,750, which means your counter would be $51,750, and you should round that up to $52,000. That's above your minimum acceptable salary of $50,000, so you will counter that amount. Not only might you get a little more than your minimum acceptable salary, but you've also left the door open to negotiate other benefits (signing bonus, vacation days, etc.) even if you end up at your minimum acceptable salary.

Scenario 2—When your counter would be less than your minimum acceptable salary: Let's say they offer $40,000. Fifteen percent of $40,000 is $6,000, which means your counter would be $46,000. That's below your minimum acceptable salary of $50,000, so you would not counter that amount. Instead, you would say, "I'm sorry, but I can't accept less than $50,000 for this job." This may very well be the end of your negotiation, so you're giving them one last shot to meet your minimum acceptable salary.

If they meet your minimum, then you've got the job at that salary. If they can't meet your minimum, then you couldn't come to terms and you should probably walk away. This can be a very difficult decision, but this specific scenario is why it was so important to set your minimum acceptable salary before you began negotiating. You were more objective then, and it's probably best to trust your objectively determined minimum in this situation.

"What if my counter seems ridiculously high?"

The nice thing about this method is that your counter is based on their initial offer, and it is confined to a reasonable range of 10% to 20% above their offer. Further, the way you chose whether to counter closer to 10% or 20% above their initial offer was based on your assessment of how badly the company needs you as compared to how badly you need the job.

A counter of 10% more than the company's initial offer simply isn't a big enough difference to raise any eyebrows. And if your counter is 20% above their initial offer, that's because you've determined that the company desperately needs you (10 out of 10 on the "How badly do they need you?" question) while *you* don't really need the job at all (0 out of 10 on the "How badly do you need this job?" question).

As long as you have realistically evaluated those two questions, your counter is in a reasonable range.

You should now have your counter ready to deliver

Congratulations! You've determined your counter, and you can feel good knowing that your method for calculating it was logical and reasonable. This is a counter that you can deliver with confidence.

Delivering your counter

When you deliver your counter, you have another opportunity to make your case for the maximum possible salary. And, more importantly, you can help the recruiter or hiring manager make a strong case to whoever is holding the purse strings. Your counter will probably require approval by someone higher up the chain of command, so you should give them everything they need to make the strongest case possible for you. Most of the time, if you're this far in the process, they want to make things work, so this is the perfect time to make your case again.

We'll approach this section as though you're going to email your counter because the best way to make your strongest case *and* make it easy for the recruiter or hiring manager to share that case with the final approver is to make it in writing.

If you absolutely can't give your counter via email, you should still write the email so that you can use it for reference when you verbally deliver your counter.

So how do you make your case to justify your counter? You already did! In the Preparation section of this chapter, there's a sub-section called "1. Why are you a valuable candidate for this job?" That's your case. You've probably already made it once—verbally to the recruiter—and you're going to make it one more time, in writing.

Here's a real example of a counter email I sent for a job I landed. I've changed some details (names, numbers), but this is almost exactly what I sent. I've tried to scale the numbers so that the proportions are about the same as the real numbers. You can also find this example at FearlessSalaryNegotiation.com/extras.

To: Brittany Jones <brittany.jones@example.com> [recruiter]
CC: Katherine Thompson <katherine.thompson@example.com> [recruiter's manager]

Subject: Josh Doody - My thoughts on Tom's verbal offer

Hi Brittany

I hope you had a great weekend!

I've been considering Tom's offer over the weekend and everything sounds good, although I would like to discuss the base salary component.

I think I'm a particularly good match for this position, where I would add significant value to ACME Corp. and to the Tom's Practice from Day One. I have a strong technical background and have built and managed teams of technical people. I am exceptionally good with clients, and have taught short courses on building rapport with and managing clients. I have an MBA and have successfully managed many portfolios of business in the Widget Making industry over the past seven years. I've been working with [Partner Company] for over two and a half years, and have experience with many of their partnership managers and leadership team. I have a strong technical writing background and can both create and delegate the creation of good collateral quickly and efficiently.

All of these qualities contribute directly to the core components of this particular position, and that's why I'm excited for the opportunity to work with Tom and his Practice in this capacity at

---

ACME Corp.

Tom offered $50,000 and I would be more comfortable if we could settle on $56,000. I feel that amount reflects the importance and expectations of the position for ACME Corp's business, and my qualifications and experience as they relate to this particular position.

Thanks for your time, and I look forward to talking with you on Monday morning at 10:30 ET!

All the best

Josh Doody
josh@example.com

Let's look a little closer.

I open with a greeting (I'm emailing the recruiter I've been working with throughout the hiring process), then immediately cut to the chase because I want this to show up in the email preview pane if possible: I'm pretty happy with the offer, but I want to talk about the base salary component. Then I immediately jump into making my case, which I initially put together during the preparation phase of this process and delivered verbally in my post-interview follow-up call with the recruiter.

Next, I summarize the verbal offer the hiring manager made, and state my preferred counter in a neutral way. I make one more one-sentence case for myself, confirm when I'll have my next phone call with the recruiter, politely signoff, and include my signature.

Notice that my counter is 12% above their initial offer, implying that my aggression factor was only a 2. In this case, I rated "How badly do they need me?" at about an 8, but I rated "How badly do I need this job?" at about a 6 because I was anxious to make a change.

I recommend that you compose an email like the one above, then send it to a couple friends or family members for review. They'll probably find some typos and might suggest some ways you can tighten it up or make it better. You can always redact the actual numbers if you're not comfortable sharing them.

Once you're happy with your counter and you feel you've made a strong case to justify it, send it to the recruiter.

After you've made your counter

So now you've made a counter and extended the negotiating window up from their offer to your counter. The recruiter will almost certainly say, "Okay, I'll need to go talk to Finance about this and see what we can do." In that case, you can jump to preparing for the final discussion. They may also say, "Okay, we can do that!" and you're done (and congrats, by the way!).

Occasionally, they'll say, "Oh no, we can't do that. The best we can do is [some number]." They've just bumped you straight to the final discussion. Fortunately, you read this whole chapter before you started negotiating, so you already have your plan for the final discussion. But for now, we'll treat it like a separate part of the process.

5. Preparing for the final discussion

You did your homework and waited for the company to make the initial offer without disclosing your current or desired salary. Then you carefully considered your counter, trying to maximize your salary while accounting for how badly the company needs you to do this job, and how badly you need this job. The recruiter may have then gone back to Finance or the hiring manager to talk about your counter and get final authorization for the amount they can pay you to do this job.

Defining the negotiation window

That conversation with Finance or the hiring manager usually goes something like this:

"We offered Josh $50,000 and he countered at $56,000. This job pays up to $58,000, so we're getting close to the top of that range. Where do we want to come back to him? Let's go with..."

They offered me $50,000 and I countered at $56,000. For now, let's just drop all the dollar signs and zeros: they offered 50 and I countered at 56. It's extremely unlikely they would come back with a number lower than 50 (after all *they* offered that number to start) or above 56 (it would be odd for them to give me more than I asked for in my counter), so they'll either stick to 50, come up to my counter of 56, or come back with something in between. This means my expected negotiation window is 50 to 56.

We'll keep using the example above for the rest of this section, but you'll want to use your own numbers to make this as relevant as possible for your own negotiation. Before you move on, you need to determine your own negotiation window so that you can plan for it. Got it? Okay, let's make a plan for each increment within your negotiation window.

Planning for each increment within your negotiation window

Now you have to do some planning for different hypotheticals. We'll make this easy by writing these down so you don't forget, and so you don't have to do much thinking during your final discussion.

The first thing to do is determine whether there's a number in your negotiation window that will make you happy such that you'll just accept that number or anything above it. In my example above, I would be happy with 55 or above, so if they responded to my counter with an offer of $55,000 or more, I would accept it and stop negotiating.

Next, you need to determine your minimum acceptable salary within the negotiation window. Note that this is not necessarily your "minimum acceptable salary" from earlier in the chapter. This may be a new number that you decide based on the window you have defined between their offer and your counter. You're updating your minimum based on what you've learned from the offer they made you.

In my case, my minimum acceptable number was 52. This means that if their response to my counter is anything below 52, I'll go straight to, "I'm sorry, but I can't accept anything less than 52 for this job."

That should leave you with some numbers below "automatic yes" and above "automatic no". This range should actually be pretty narrow by now, and you can probably break it into a few $1,000 or $500 increments. For each increment, you'll prepare a salary request, plus a benefits request. The salary request is a number that you can give in the following way: "If you can meet me at this amount, I'm on board." The benefits request is in case they can't meet you at that amount; you'll want to ask about other "levers" you can pull as part of your benefits package. List these so that the most important ones are first.

Which levers you want to pull in your benefits request are up to you, but you should have at least two or three in mind because some things are set in stone at some companies while others may be negotiable. In fact, *everything* except salary may be set in stone, but at least you can try to eke out some additional benefits once you've found the maximum salary they will pay you. Some benefits that may be negotiable include vacation days, work location (maybe you can work from home two days a week to reduce your commute), greater reimbursements for home-office costs (home internet, office lease), reimbursement for your mobile phone if you'll use it for work, reimbursement for relocation expenses, and so on.

Let's make this easy and just write down a reaction to each number from 50 through 56:

> **56**—That sounds good to me! When do I start?
> **55**—That sounds good to me! When do I start?
> **53.5 to 54**—(1) I'm on board if you can do 55. (2) Can we talk about upping my vacation? (3) Can we talk about reimbursing my monthly office expenses ($265)?
> **52.5 to 53**—(1) I'm on board if you can do 54.5. (2) Vacation. (3) Office expenses.
> **51.5 to 52**—(1) I'm on board if you can do 54. (2) Vacation. (3) Office expenses.
> **51**—I can't accept less than 52.
> **50**—I can't accept less than 52.

Once you've written out your script, you're ready for your final discussion.

How this tactic earned me $1,500

I realize this may seem like overkill, but it's absolutely worth the effort. In fact, this method saved me $1,500 in the real-life negotiation that's the basis for our example.

The final discussion will often be verbal, and most people (myself included) tend to get nervous when negotiating something high-stakes in real-time. This method helps you run through the possibilities for your final discussion ahead of time and script your responses so that stress isn't as much of a factor.

When I was negotiating the salary we've been using for this example, the recruiter called me for the final discussion, and she gave me their response to my counter. Their response was 53.5.

I was nervous, so my mind jumped straight to thinking, "You didn't get the salary you countered with, so let's try for some additional benefits." I started to say, "Okay, can we talk about what other levers might be available to pull in terms of benefits...." But then I looked up at my whiteboard and realized that "No! That's not the first thing I say if they say 53.5!" The white board said that the first thing I should say if they responded with 53.5 was, "If you can do 55, then I'm on board." So, I stopped myself and said, "Actually, forget I said that. If you can do 55, then I'm on board."

The recruiter said, "Okay, I think we can do that. I just need to get it approved." and our call was over about 20 seconds later. I almost settled for $53,500 as my base salary, but because I had a script prepared for the final discussion, I earned an extra $1,500.

6. Final discussion

The company made you an offer and you asked for some time to think it over. Then you countered, hopefully in an email that also made a strong case for why your skillset and experience are valuable to the company. The company will likely take some time to discuss things internally and determine how high they want to go within the window that has been established between their offer and your counter. Once they've determined how far they can go, they'll usually reach out for one more discussion. The final discussion is almost always a phone call, but will sometimes be by email.

You should have your script from the previous section ready to go because the final discussion will probably move quickly. You'll exchange greetings, then the recruiter or hiring manager will let you know that they've discussed your counter internally and they're prepared to offer some amount. You can't know that exact amount before they say it out loud, but that's okay because you've already written a script that covers most of their possible responses.

Once they react to your counter, your next response will often end the negotiation. You'll either say, "I'm sorry, I just can't accept an offer that low. The absolute lowest I can accept is [your minimum acceptable number]." Or you'll say, "That's pretty close, and if we can settle on [some number], I'm on board right now." Or you'll say, "That sounds good to me! Let's do it!" This is all in your script.

When they respond to the "...if we can settle on [some number], I'm on board right now" by saying, "We can't come up that far. The best we can do is [their final offer]", then you can try to get some other benefits by asking if there are other levers that can be adjusted. Here is how you might ask about those other benefits:

"Okay, so the best you can do on base salary is [their final offer]. Can we talk about what other levers might be available in terms of other benefits?"

Some of those levers might be vacation days, work location, reimbursements, signing bonus, start date, or whatever you listed in your script when you prepared for the final discussion. Once you've tried to get those other benefits, you'll have a clear picture of your best-case scenario and can either accept their final offer or not.

If the negotiation ends and you won't be joining the company, that's okay because it means the company simply couldn't offer you the minimum amount you would be willing to accept for this job. This is ultimately a good outcome because it means that you didn't wind up with a job where the pay isn't sufficient for your needs. Send a short thank-you email to the recruiter, including your contact information, to make sure everything is amicable. Be sure to let them know they can reach out to you any time if they find another opportunity that may be a good fit for you.

If you were able to come to an agreement, congratulations! The recruiter or hiring manager probably has the next action to get final approval for your offer and confirm your start date, so just hang back and wait for things to take shape.

Summary

Many people relax once they have a job offer, often because they're so relieved to be through with the interview process and to have something tangible to show for it. Don't relax! This is an opportunity to maximize your pay at your new job.

The theory behind my strategy

By learning as much as you can about the job being offered and the current market conditions, and by being bold, you can often significantly improve your financial situation during the negotiation process.

Remember that although this negotiation may be a unique and special event for you personally, it's just a series of numbers to most recruiters. Your task is to get the largest salary the recruiter is prepared to offer—don't short-change yourself.

Focus on base salary

Base salary is the number that really matters. "Total comp" is a bigger number, but includes many more variables, most of which are out of your control. So focus your negotiation on maximizing your base salary.

The general phases of salary negotiation with a new company

1. Preparation
2. Post-interview follow-up
3. Initial offer
4. Your counter
5. Preparing for the final discussion
6. Final discussion

1. Preparation

You have two main objectives before you begin negotiating:

1. Understand why you are a valuable candidate for this job
2. Determine the minimum salary you require to do this job

This is where you do your homework and make *sure* you're ready to make a case for yourself. Think about and write down your response to each of these things:

1. Why are you a valuable candidate for this job?

This is extremely subjective, but you've spent enough time researching and discussing this particular job that you should be able to identify what your most valuable attributes are as they relate to the job and the company.

You can bolster your case by building some attribute-for-need combinations that you can use to describe how valuable you can be for this company. Here's an example:

"You're building a team of salespeople and solutions architects to grow into the medical manufacturing vertical, and I have five years of experience in sales in that vertical. I can help you grow more efficiently and focus on the right things from the beginning."

2. What is the minimum salary you require to do this job?

Here are several things you should consider as you determine the absolute minimum salary you'll accept to do this job:

- **Your current salary**
- **Your market value for this job**
- **The amount you think you can get**

- **What people in that job at that company are currently making** CAUTION: Do not mention this during your negotiation!
- **How badly do they need you? (0–10)** If it's a high number, emphasize this during your negotiation.
- **How badly do you need this job? (0–10)** If it's a low number, emphasize this during your negotiation.
- **When is your next merit increase at your current job?**
- **When is your next bonus at your current job?**

Picking a number: The absolute minimum salary you will accept before walking away from the opportunity

This is the most important number you'll take into your negotiation, and it's important that you decide on this number *before* you begin negotiating. Choose your minimum acceptable salary and write it down.

2. Post-interview follow-up

The post-interview follow-up is typically a short, verbal discussion with the recruiter or hiring manager. They're just letting you know that you're finished interviewing and they are considering next steps, including making you an offer.

You have two objectives for this call:

1. Don't give the first number in your salary negotiation.
2. Make your best case that you will be a valuable asset to the company and that they should make as strong an offer as possible.

The recruiter will often ask you something like this in order to elicit a desired salary from you:

"Okay, I just need to talk to Finance and your hiring manager to see whether we're ready to move forward with an offer. What

sort of salary did you have in mind for this job? I just want to have something to run by Finance. And do you have any questions for me before we move forward?"

Here is a good response that gives you an opportunity to make your case for the maximum salary they can offer:

"You know, I really don't have a specific number in mind right now. I've learned a lot through the interview process, and I look forward to hearing what you suggest so I can consider it. As I mentioned earlier in this process, I want this move to be a big step forward for me in terms of both responsibility and compensation because I know I can immediately contribute to help you address [this need] with [this positive attribute], and [this other need] with [this other positive attribute]."

3. Initial offer

The recruiter or hiring manager will usually deliver your Initial offer either verbally (a phone call) or via email. Either way, your response should be something like:

"Thank you so much for the offer. I would like to take a day or two to think it over before I respond."

If it helps, mention that you need to talk it over with your spouse or family. You just want to get the offer and then take some time to work on your counter. You're not negotiating, accepting, or rejecting the offer yet.

4. Your counter

Even if you really like the offer, you may still want to negotiate for a higher salary because it's possible that you previously under-valued yourself. Before you determine your counter, you should reevaluate what you learned in the preparation phase to make sure you don't need to update any of your answers to those questions.

Before you can determine your counter, you need to calculate your aggression factor. The formula is very simple:

[How badly they need you] - [How badly you need this job]
= Your aggression factor

If your aggression factor works out to be less than zero, just set it to 0. That means your aggression factor should always be a number between 0 and 10.

Determining your counter

A good range for a counter is between 10% and 20% above their initial offer. On the low end, 10% is enough to make a counter worthwhile, but not enough to cause anyone any heartburn. On the high end, 20% is a pretty big difference between their offer and your counter, but it's not so big that it will come across as excessive when used in the right situation.

You will encounter two primary scenarios:

1. When they offer at least your minimum acceptable salary: We need to determine where in the typical counter range—between 10% and 20%—you should counter. This is where your aggression factor comes into play. You just add your aggression factor to 10% and that's how much you should counter above their offer. In our example above, your aggression factor was 5, so your counter would be 15% above their initial offer (10% plus 5% for your aggression factor).

For example, say that your minimum acceptable salary is $50,000 and the company offered you $55,000. They met your minimum, so now you just need to determine an appropriate counter. Your aggression factor is a 5, which means your counter should be 15% above their offer. In this case, 15% of $55,000 is $8,250, which means your counter should be $63,250. It can be a little easier to work with rounder numbers, so you might round up to $63,500.

2. When they offer less than your minimum acceptable salary: Use the method in the previous section to determine what your counter would be. If that number is greater than your minimum acceptable salary, then that is your counter. If that number is less than or equal to your minimum acceptable salary, just tell the recruiter or hiring manager that you can't accept less than your minimum acceptable salary.

If they meet or exceed your minimum, then you're all set; if they can't meet your minimum, then you couldn't come to terms and you should probably walk away.

Delivering your counter

This is yet another opportunity to make your case for the maximum salary possible. You want to deliver your counter along with solid evidence that supports what you're asking for to make it as easy as possible for whoever needs to approve the final salary to get on board.

Regardless of whether you're delivering your counter via email or verbally, write an email similar to the example I provided earlier in the chapter. The email has everything you need to make your case for the maximum salary possible. You'll either deliver it as an email so that it can be forwarded or shared internally, or you'll review the email and use its content as a guide for a verbal discussion when you deliver your counter.

The email should be short, sweet, and to the point:

- Greeting
- A brief description of what you want to change (usually base salary)
- A list of reasons your request is reasonable (your attribute-for-need combinations)
- Restate the original offer and then state your counter
- Confirm when you'll next talk about your counter
- Neutral Signoff and Signature

Once you've delivered your counter, the recruiter will likely take some time to discuss it internally and build a response. In the meantime, you'll be preparing for your final discussion.

5. Preparing for the final discussion

It's extremely important to thoroughly prepare for the final discussion because it will often be verbal, and it will be easy to make mistakes and miss opportunities in the heat of the moment. Instead, you'll script your responses so that you're ready for pretty much every response they may have to your counter.

Once you have made your counter, you essentially have defined the window in which you are negotiating. The bottom of the window is their offer and the top of the window is your counter. There are a discrete number of salaries (probably in $1,000 or $500 increments) that can really be listed in that window, so you'll treat each of those as a hypothetical and determine your response if they come back with each salary in the window.

First, determine the number that you would be happy with—your "automatic yes" number. Next, determine the minimum number you'll accept—your "automatic no" number. You won't just say "no", you'll say, "I can't come on board for anything less than [this number]."

Now you've narrowed the window even further to those numbers between "automatic yes" and "automatic no". This should leave you with just a few increments, and you'll write down your response to each increment with the following two pieces:

1. A number that you can give in the following way: "If you can meet me at this amount, I'm on board."
2. If they can't meet you at that amount, you'll want to ask about other levers you can pull as part of your benefits package. List these so that the most important ones are first.

Now you have your "automatic yes" and "automatic no" numbers, and you have a scripted response for each number in between. You're ready for your final discussion.

6. Final discussion

This discussion will be quick. The recruiter or hiring manager will respond to your counter, and you'll use your script to determine your next move. Once you make that next move, that usually will be it, or there will be some haggling over small benefits (vacation, moving expenses, etc.).

When your conversation ends, you'll either have a tentative agreement in place (often pending approval by the company), or you will have realized that the company simply cannot meet your minimum acceptable salary and you won't be joining them. Either way, this is a good result for you.

Thank the recruiter for their time and ask about next steps. If you couldn't come to an agreement, make sure the recruiter has your contact information in case they want to reach out in the future. If they're sending a formal offer, just hang back and wait for it.

CHAPTER 5

How to leave a job on the best possible terms

Leaving a job isn't nearly as exciting as *getting* or *starting* one, but it's just as important. After your first job, every job you start will be preceded by one you left. And, more importantly, you'll get many of your jobs through contacts from previous jobs.

Sometimes, you'll leave a job because you found a much better opportunity, and you're really excited about starting a new chapter in your career. Sometimes, you'll leave because you were laid off, or fired, or because it just wasn't a good fit for you. Regardless of why you're leaving, the most important thing is that you do it gracefully. Why? Because people know people, and they talk to people, and they will talk about *you*. And when they talk about you, you want to be absolutely sure that they only have great things to say.

So how do you make sure that people only have great things to say about you after you leave a job? Here are some general principles that you should review every time you leave a job. Do these things and people will think very highly of you after you've left.

Getting let go from my second full-time job

My second job was a good job at a small, private company, and I was surrounded by good people. And then, six weeks later, we were acquired by a mid-sized public company. A couple years later, that company was acquired by a private equity firm, taken private, and the overhaul began. There was a round of layoffs every few months, and it became pretty obvious my team wasn't safe. Eventually, they let most of my team go and I experienced my first layoff.

I was obviously frustrated, but what was done was done. I asked my boss what I could do to help button everything up before I left. I tied up a lot of loose ends, and generally went out of my way to make sure the project I had been working on for the past six months was well documented and ready for whoever would take it over. I left on excellent terms and didn't say anything foolish on my way out the door.

Fortunately, I had a little money saved up, and my company gave me a decent severance package. I spent the next few months sort of looking for work, and generally enjoying unemployment. I had no idea what I would do next, but at least I had some time to think about it.

Landing my third full-time job

About three months later, I got a call from a manager at the company that had recently laid me off. I had never met him before, but he had heard about me: "Josh, I'm building a Support team in Gainesville. So far, it's just me, but we're establishing a Gainesville headquarters. I was wondering if you'd be interested in helping me build the team. I've heard really good things about you and I think you would be a good fit."

This was surprising for a few reasons. First, I had never worked with the product this team would be supporting. I had worked at the company, but in a totally different area. Second, I had *no* meaningful experience in Support. I had worked in a couple call centers right after high school, but those jobs hadn't been on my résumé in many years. Third, I'd never been a manager or hired anyone. I wouldn't technically be a manager in the new role, but I would be directly responsible for interviewing and making go/no-go recommendations for hiring people to build out the team.

So, why did he call me? It was a combination of two things: my reputation for taking on new challenges and, more importantly, because I had been very careful to leave on good terms without burning any bridges when I had been laid off.

While at the company the first time, I had worked hard to contribute where I would be most useful. My final role was a "special project", which I knew was risky, but which the company had made a priority. When I took that role, I moved one step up the company's org chart, took on more responsibility, and took on a lot more risk. This earned me a reputation as a guy who could be counted on to take on new challenges, even if the payoff was uncertain.

But that wouldn't have mattered if I had left the company on bad terms. There were a lot of things I could've said or done on my way out that would've been very cathartic. They *had* laid me off, after all. And after I had taken on an important special project to boot! But I was careful to leave on good terms, to tie up loose ends, and to make sure my previous project was well documented for my successor. That was at least as important as my prior reputation.

I would eventually get two more jobs because of my reputation with that company. I didn't pursue either of them—they both found me.

Leave on the best possible terms, even if you feel slighted

Ask your manager and co-workers what you can help with before you go

I was let go during the third round of layoffs that year. Earlier the same year, in the second round of layoffs, a very reliable co-worker (let's call him Jim) was let go. They gave him the bad news in the morning, and told him he had until the end of the day to clear everything out and wrap things up. He immediately emailed my boss and me—he had been supporting us on that special project— to let us know he had been let go. But, more importantly, he also told us he was working to give us credentials to all the servers, databases, folders, etc., that we would need to take everything off his plate. He even put together a document with passwords, URLs, network addresses, instructions, etc. He left us a full manual to use once he was gone.

He didn't have to do that. He could've just said, "Well, I guess that's it for me," powered down his laptop and signed off for the day. No one would've faulted him for just clocking out and leaving the rest of us to fend for ourselves. Instead, he took care to make sure his co-workers had everything they needed to continue his projects in his absence.

But that's not the end of the story. A few years later, a friend of mine heard that Jim was looking for a job and had applied to her company. "Do you remember Jim? He's looking for work and just applied at my company. What do you think?" I said, "Hire him immediately!" Then I told her the story I just told you. Jim had been very good at his job, but he had also demonstrated exceptional character and reliability in the worst of circumstances. He's working for my friend's company now and he's a superstar.

Document the projects you're working on to prepare your successor

The best anecdote I have for this one is the same one I just shared with you. Jim is the prototype here—do what he did.

Bundle up relevant documentation, emails, etc., and save them somewhere others can get to them

In 2014, I decided it was time for a change, and I moved on to a new company and a new opportunity. Before I left, I found out who would be replacing me on each of my projects, and I sent them a .zip file with everything they would need to know about the projects they were inheriting. I sent them documentation, relevant email trails, specs, files—anything they *might* need after I was gone. I wanted to make sure the clients I had worked with would perceive the transition to be silky smooth.

A few months later, I heard through the grapevine that one of my old projects was having some trouble. Nobody could find the contract and statement of work, and they needed those documents to resolve some discrepancies between the client's and company's interpretation of the project's scope.

I had worked on that project for a year, but it pre-dated me by about 18 months. When I first inherited it, I ran into similar issues locating the contract, statement of work, and other documentation describing our responsibilities and deliverables for the project. So I spent a Saturday morning looking for all that documentation and bundling it up.

"I sent all that stuff to Ben before I left. Tell him to look for an email from me in March. There should be a big .zip file attached to it, and the client's name is in the subject. The contract and SOW are in that .zip file." A few days later, I got word that everything was there, just like I said. If I hadn't sent that .zip file, that information may have been lost forever. I saved the company a lot of grief and managed to bolster my reputation at the same time.

Even if your company already has everything stored in the cloud, you can still put together a single document that points to everything your successor will need.

Make sure to quickly return all your equipment in good shape

If your company loaned you a laptop, mobile phone, headset, monitor, keyboard, printer, iPad or other equipment, make sure you ask what you need to return, and how you can return it. Many companies will tell you to just keep some stuff (especially printers), but don't assume you should keep anything. Assume you should return everything, and only keep things they explicitly tell you to keep.

And think about the IT person who will receive that box. Don't just randomly throw a bunch of stuff in there and ship it. Be sure to include a Post-It with your laptop password, your mobile phone PIN, and other bits of information they may need to access those devices and reset them. Ask yourself, "If I had to open this box and process all this stuff, how would I want it to be packaged?" and do that.

Reach out to your closest co-workers before you leave to make sure they're part of your network

You should also reach out to your closest co-workers—the ones you would IM to make snarky jokes when something funny happened—and personally tell them that you're leaving. They may feel slighted if they don't hear from you, and you want to leave on the best possible terms.

While you're reaching out to your closest co-workers, make sure you have their personal contact information so you can keep in touch. They may be the ones who find a big opportunity for you later on, and you want to make sure they can find you when they do. Your network is one of your most valuable assets when it comes to finding good opportunities, and this is a great chance to extend it before you leave.

Reach out to your colleagues to say goodbye and share your contact information

This is a pretty standard practice nowadays. Usually, people put together an email to their team, or practice, or department, tell them it was great working them, they'll be missed, and to reach out if they ever need anything. This is about 50% genuine and 50% networking.

The genuine part is that you're giving your former co-workers a way to find you if they run into an issue with one of your old responsibilities. The networking part is that you're sharing your name, email address and phone number so that your co-workers have your contact info in case they find an awesome job you would be right for.

Here's a short example you can use to say goodbye and make sure your former co-workers know how to find you if they need to. This is a real email—slightly modified—that I sent when I left a great job in 2015. You can also find this example at FearlessSalaryNegotiation.com/extras.

To: ACME Corp—Consulting Practice
CC: Josh Doody <josh@example.com> [personal email address]

Subject: See you around!

Hi everyone

Today is my last day working with this amazing team at this amazing company. It has been a pleasure working with all of you, and I'm grateful for the opportunity to work with such a great team of experts. The amount of talent in this group is really astounding.

I've been in this industry for almost 10 years now, and I've learned that this is a very tight-knit industry where I continuously bump into old friends. I'm sure we'll cross paths again, and that's very comforting given how great this team is.

If you ever need anything or have any questions for me about any of my projects or responsibilities please reach out and ask. Don't spin your wheels trying to figure something out when you could just email me for a quick answer!

And of course, please stay in touch and feel free to reach out at any time to say hello.

My personal email address is: josh@example.com
I'm on LinkedIn at: https://www.linkedin.com/in/joshdoody

Thank you for this tremendous opportunity, and for making this such a fantastic place to work!

All the best

Josh

Be vague and use positive language in your exit interview

When I left my first job, I was frustrated and a little disillusioned. I didn't think my boss had helped me find opportunities I wanted, and I realized that my own performance didn't matter.

So I started looking for a new job in a new industry. I applied for two jobs and landed one pretty quickly. Adios, old job!

I gave notice and began ticking off the list of things I had to do before I left: wrap up open projects, say goodbye to friends and colleagues... complete an online exit interview? What's that? I looked it over and saw that the company wanted me to give them anonymous feedback about my experience and tell them why I was leaving.

Ah ha! It's ANONYMOUS?! The perfect opportunity to tell them how I really feel! I'll tell them all about this crummy assignment I had to do, and how my boss wouldn't give me any cool opportunities and... Hmm. I wonder who will read this? To Google!

Google told me to cool my jets—the exit interview is not the place to let off steam or, as my friend Rob would say, "go out in a blaze of glory". So I backed off and gave some general feedback—hard to find interesting projects, considering a career change, that sort of thing—without going into too much detail.

It wasn't very satisfying, but Google said it was the prudent thing to do.

On my last day, I stopped by my boss' office to give him my badge and say goodbye.

I sat down across from him, and he reached out and picked up a small stack of papers. "So I read your exit interview..." *What? That was supposed to be anonymous!* I panicked a little bit, remembering what I wanted to say on that form. Then I remembered that I had backed off and sanitized everything I wrote. "...It's too bad we couldn't find something more challenging for you, but I'm sure you'll find something you enjoy at your next job."

Well, that could've been awkward. If I had written what I really wanted to say in the exit interview, our final conversation could have gone much differently.

Things to consider when completing an exit interview

I'll leave you with three specific things to consider when completing an exit interview:

- **DO focus on yourself and your own needs.** "I'm ready for a new challenge" or "I found a new opportunity that I think will be a good fit for me." This way, you can give the company some insight into your decision without pointing any fingers. This is easier if you focus on using positive language.
- **DON'T focus on others or the company.** Don't say things like, "The company culture just wore me down" or "My boss didn't give me enough support." It might feel good at the time, but probably won't change anything and could hurt you later. This is easier if you avoid negative language.
- **DO remember that the exit interview will likely stay in your file, and may be read by others at the company.** If I had been harsh in my exit interview, what could have happened? What might my old boss say if he was called to verify my previous employment? He probably wouldn't explicitly mention the exit interview, but he might hesitate when answering questions about me. That wouldn't be good.

Summary

Leaving a job is as important as starting one. It's a final opportunity to leave a positive impression on your co-workers and build a bridge from one job to another, as opposed to burning the bridge behind you on your way out.

When you leave a job, be conscientious, focusing on the needs of the co-workers you're leaving behind. Leave on good terms and make sure you button things up so that whoever picks up where you left off will have an easy time of it.

Leaving a job properly can go a very long way to boosting your reputation so that you're top of mind when your former co-workers are looking for new colleagues in the future.

A short summary of things to do when leaving a job

Leave on the best possible terms, even if you feel slighted

It's always difficult to put on a happy face when things aren't going well, but this is a time when you can really boost your reputation.

Ask your manager and co-workers what you can help with before you go

Do this and you will make a lasting impression on your co-workers.

Document the projects you're working on to prepare your successor

Your successor will have a much easier time absorbing your work, and they'll thank you for it.

Bundle up relevant documentation, emails, etc., and save them somewhere others can get to them

Most companies are moving to cloud-based storage, so it may all be out there anyway. Even so, put together a master document that points to everything they'll need.

Make sure to quickly return all your equipment in good shape

Most of the time, you are just borrowing company property. You should return it in good shape, just like you would want your own property returned if you lent it out.

Reach out to your closest co-workers before you leave to make sure they're part of your network

Your network is one of your most valuable assets for finding future career opportunities.

Reach out to your colleagues to say goodbye and share your contact information

If you've done all these things, you've left a great impression. Make sure your old co-workers know how to find you if they need someone like you in the future. And be sure to reach out to your closest co-workers to personally say goodbye whenever possible.

Be vague and use positive language in your exit interview

Your exit interview is one of the times when being vague is necessary. You won't benefit by baring your soul on your way out, and the company isn't going to change because of your feedback. Keep it short, sweet, and surface-level.

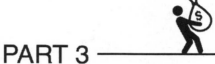

——————— PART 3 ———————

Getting paid what you're worth within your current company

Do you have to quit your job to get a big raise?

It's common knowledge that the way to get big pay increases is to change jobs. But is that really your only option?

The answer depends on how your company handles raises and promotions. Some companies are very rigid when it comes to pay increases—merit increases are almost always in a well-defined range, and promotions come with predetermined raise amounts depending on how many pay grades you advance. Other companies are much more fluid and have fewer restrictions in place when it comes to employee pay.

So it's possible you'll need to change jobs to get a big raise, but it's also possible you can get a pretty big raise by staying put and playing your cards right.

First, let's set a baseline for raise sizing:

- Small raise: 1%
- Normal raise: 2-3%
- Good raise: 4-7%
- Big raise: 8%+

In my experience, these ranges are pretty accurate, but they may vary depending on which industry you're in and other factors.

The trouble with shooting for a big raise or promotion during merit increase time

Most companies have an annual merit cycle, sometimes based on the calendar year, and sometimes based on the company's fiscal year. The merit cycle often ends with performance reviews, a small merit increase, and maybe even a bonus. Most employees assume the best (or only) time to get a raise or promotion is during that short period at the end of the merit cycle.

In fact, this is often a *bad* time to hope for a big pay increase because the merit increases (including promotions) are often budgeted ahead of time, and that budget is shared by a team, department, or even the entire company. That means many people are vying for their piece of a shared budget. If you get a big raise, it means someone else will likely get a small raise, or no raise at all. This puts a lot of pressure on managers to try to distribute their piece of that pie evenly across their team members so that everyone gets something and is at least somewhat happy.

The result is that it's often extremely difficult to get a big raise or paid promotion during the regular merit increase period.

Shoot for an off-cycle raise or promotion

So what can you do? Your best option may be an "off-cycle" raise or promotion. These are often handled as one-off events, which means they're not necessarily pulled from a fixed pool of money, and they're evaluated individually from a finance perspective.

A well-timed request for an off-cycle raise or promotion can often give you the best shot at a nice pay increase because you're not competing with everyone else in the company for a fixed amount of money. Instead, you can make your case as an individual who has earned greater pay or a better title.

Off-cycle raises and promotions carry the added benefit that they usually don't affect your on-cycle raise potential. So, you'll usually still be eligible for whatever merit increase you would have already been eligible for during the regular merit increase period.

Sometimes there's just nothing you can do

Still, there are some companies where everything is pre-determined, including raises and promotions. At these companies, it can be extremely difficult to get a big raise.

For example, I worked at a company where it was expressly written that a one-pay-grade promotion came with a 4% raise, and a two-pay-grade promotion came with a 7% raise. Of course, 7% isn't "nothing", but it's not exactly a big payday, especially considering the big jump in title and responsibility.

At that company, I realized my potential earnings were more or less predetermined, and the only way I would get a big pay increase was to leave and go to another company. So that's what I did.

Things to find out when determining your potential for a big raise

I'll leave you with a few specific things to help you determine if you can get a big raise without leaving your current job. You can usually ask your manager about these things, or you may find information in your company's employee handbook or from co-workers who have recently been promoted.

- **_You_ can initiate the conversation.** Many people assume that raises and promotions will come to them over time. That may be true, but you may be missing opportunities for more pay if you don't talk to your manager about your options.
- **Is there a fixed budget for raises and promotions during the normal merit increase cycle?** If there is, it can be very difficult for any one person to get a big raise during the normal merit increase cycle because so many people are vying for a piece of a fixed-budget pie. You may be better off waiting to shoot for an off-cycle promotion instead.
- **Is an off-cycle promotion or raise an option?** Many companies treat off-cycle promotions and raises as unique events, evaluated one at a time. This means an off-cycle promotion may give you an opportunity to make your case and push for a larger raise based on your experience and value to the company.
- **If a promotion would mean moving to a new job at your company, are there any posted openings for that job?** If you're a Project Manager and your next promotion would be to Portfolio Manager (rather than something like Project Manager II), you may want to start by checking your company's jobs board to see if there are any positions open for that job. If there are, you can specifically target a promotion to that job. If there aren't, you may have to see whether you can simply shoot for an off-cycle raise (without a promotion), or you may need to start looking at other companies if you want to move up.

- **Are the pay increases for promotions predetermined?** Sometimes it doesn't matter when you get a raise or promotion—your potential is predetermined. In these cases, getting a "big" raise is very, very difficult and you'll need to consider moving to a new company if that is important to you.

This should help you determine if you can get a big raise by staying put, or if you may need to start looking elsewhere.

Let's walk through the process for getting a promotion or a raise at your current company.

CHAPTER 6

How to get your next promotion

Requesting a promotion can be intimidating. Here are some common reasons you might use to talk yourself out of asking for a promotion, along with my response to each:

- **I don't even know how to ask for a promotion. Do I ask in person? Through email?** We'll cover this in detail. You will start by asking in person, then follow up with an email—I'll walk you through both.
- **What if my manager says no?** I'm going to help you put together a very strong case to minimize this possibility. But even if your manager does say no, that's okay because you can still say, "Okay, I understand. Can you help me understand *why I'm not ready* for a promotion so that I know what to work on?"
- **Do I deserve a promotion?** It's not about the time you put in, but the value you add to your company. I will help you demonstrate that you've *earned* a promotion.
- **Don't I just need to work harder and harder until I get a promotion?** It would be nice if it were this simple, but this just isn't how companies work.
- **Don't I have to wait until my next performance review?** Nope!

What about raises? At the end of this chapter, I'll cover the very general "standard raise" that often accompanies a promotion. My assumption is that a promotion really contains two components: a title change and a consummate increase in pay. This isn't always true, but it's the case most of the time. As I mentioned in "Do you have to quit your job to get a big raise?", many companies have a rubric they use to determine the specific raise amount that accompanies a promotion, so this chapter assumes some sort of rubric will be used to determine the raise that should accompany your promotion at your company.

In the next chapter, "How to get your next raise", I'll talk about requesting a raise to bring your compensation into alignment with your market value. So if you're not looking for a title change, and are just looking for a "market adjustment" or more money for your current role, you may want to jump to that chapter. If you're looking for a title change *and* a market adjustment, just keep reading through this chapter and the next.

Okay, back to promotions! When you ask for a promotion, you're asking that your title and salary be adjusted to reflect the increased value you are adding to the company since you began working in your current role. That "increase in value" may be that you're managing more people, taking on bigger projects, creating collateral that others are using to be more efficient at their jobs, doing things outside your current job description, or any number of other things that you weren't doing before.

Notice I didn't say "...increased value you *might* add to the company..." or "...you *will* add to the company..." I said "...the increased value you *are adding* to the company..." Companies generally don't promote people based on potential—they promote based on *results*.

Let's look at the high-level process for earning a promotion. It's pretty simple:

1. Define your goal
2. Produce results to show you're ready
3. Document your accomplishments and accolades
4. Prepare your case
5. Present your case

The goal of this chapter is that once you present your case, it'll be such a good case for a promotion that your manager and her manager, plus the Finance person who has to approve things, will be impressed and immediately see that you're doing your target job, so they'll say, "Well, it seems like he's already doing the job, so let's make it official and promote him!" Or, at the very least, you'll understand that although you feel that you've already demonstrated your readiness for a promotion, your company simply can't accommodate you, so you'll either need to put a plan in place to achieve your goal, or you may need to look at other options.

Before you get started, I recommend that you get the tools and templates I've made to help you work through the promotion process. Get them for free at FearlessSalaryNegotiation.com/extras.

And if you prefer to learn by doing, take a look at "How to get promoted in 7 days", a companion email course for this chapter. It's a step-by-step guide that walks you through the entire promotion process in seven quick lessons. Get it for free at FearlessSalaryNegotiation.com/promotion-course.

1. Define your goal

What really matters is that you know where you want to be promoted. *Specifically*, I mean. Not "I want a promotion", but "I want to be promoted to Engineer II" or "I want to be promoted to a role in Operations." This matters because you need to know how your target role is different from your current role so that you can identify opportunities to do things associated with your target role.

There are two common types of promotion: straight-up and over-and-up.

Straight-up promotions

With a straight-up promotion, you're just moving to the next job above your current one on your career path. Most straight-up promotions look something like this:

- Engineer → Engineer II
- Associate Consultant → Consultant

If you're an Engineer, you might move up to Engineer II. If you're an Associate Consultant, you could move up to Consultant. Sometimes you'll move from an individual contributor role like Engineer III up to a managerial or supervisory role like Technical Lead.

For straight-up promotions, the easiest way to learn what makes your target job different from your current role is to compare the two job descriptions. This should be pretty easy because most job descriptions within a career path are literally copied and pasted with minor updates. By looking at the job descriptions, you can clearly see what your current job responsibilities are, and then you can see what additional responsibilities accompany the description for your target job.

Over-and-up promotions

With an over-and-up promotion, you're moving "over" into a different part of the business and "up" into a new role. Your target job might be *related* to your current job, but isn't necessarily on the same career path. If you're in Consulting, maybe you could move over and up to Product Management. If you're in Finance, you could move over and up to Operations.

It can be a little tricky to figure out the difference between your current job and your target job when you're pursuing an over-and-up promotion. If the new job you're targeting is outside your current group, run it by your manager first. You may need to explain that you're interested in a new role, and you want to get experience with it to see if it might be a good option for you in the future. Be as transparent as possible so that your manager doesn't think that you're being sneaky, and so you can avoid any political landmines that may be lurking.

Next, compare the job descriptions to see if you can identify things that your target job requires, but that your current job doesn't. If you can't find a job description for your target job, or if you're having trouble comparing your target and current jobs, you can reach out to your manager or HR to see if they have the job description or can put you in touch with a manager in that part of the company. You could also reach out to someone who's already doing your target job in that part of the company, and ask them if you can set up a 20-minute call to talk about their job—what they do, their day-to-day—so you can learn more about it.

When you're comparing your job description to the one you're targeting, don't get hung up on "years of experience"—look at everything else. Here's what you really want to know: *What does the new role require that I'm not currently doing?*

Your takeaway from this section is that you have some idea what you're shooting for (a promotion), *and* you know what you can do to demonstrate that you have already earned that promotion before you request it.

Do you want to do that job?

This may seem silly, but it's important: Now that you have a clear picture of what your target job is, do you want to do that job? If your answer is "Yep!" then you're in good shape and ready to move on to the next topic, "Produce results to show you're ready".

But if your answer is "I'm not so sure", then consider looking for other jobs that are more interesting. You could talk to your manager about other opportunities in your company, and ask for suggestions that might suit you and your skillset. Maybe your manager can suggest some jobs you might enjoy and put you in touch with other managers in that area.

Once you find a job you want to pursue, you can loop back here to "Define your goal" and do some research to determine the differences between your current job and the new job you're targeting.

2. Produce results to show you're ready

The first part of defining your goal is determining what you're after. The second part of defining your goal is determining the differences between your current job and your target job. The third part of defining your goal is to create a specific plan—a roadmap—to get experience with each of those differences to demonstrate that you're ready for this promotion.

A CEO tells me what managers look for

A few years ago, I had an opportunity to talk with the CEO of a large public utility company. We met in his office on the top floor of a tall building and we talked for 90 minutes. This was extremely generous of him—think how much his time must be worth—and I wanted to make the most of it.

Our conversation covered a lot of ground, but there's one question and answer combo that really stands out to me, even now. I asked, "How do you find the people that you promote to be your VPs and SVPs?" I wanted to know the secret sauce for finding untapped potential, for identifying future superstars so that I could get promoted myself, and so that I too would know how to find talent.

His answer was, "I look for people that are already working in and exploring areas outside their own, and I promote them." In other words, he was looking for people already doing the jobs he needed to fill.

I expected him to use words like "potential" and "future", but instead he used the word "already". I learned that business managers don't generally promote people based on *potential*, they promote them based on *results*. *They're looking for people who have already demonstrated that they can do the job.* They may have to train them on the specific details or operational duties of the new role, but the major pieces are often in place before the promotion.

In hindsight, this is obvious. Managers are very, very busy people. They don't have much time to teach people how to do new jobs. They barely have enough time to delegate and manage the business they're responsible for running. So they're not looking for *potential*, they're looking for value *right now*.

Do the job, then ask to make it official

From this perspective, a promotion looks a little different. Instead of something that's granted to you by managers when they think you're ready, it's something you do and then ask to make it official.

What does this mean for you? It means that those differences you found between your current job and the job you're pursuing are things you need to accomplish *now* to make your case for a promotion *later*. Those differences—the things you need to accomplish to demonstrate you're ready for your target job—are your roadmap to getting your next promotion. Now, you just need to start following that roadmap, putting a pin in each new skill or ability as you gain the experience you need to demonstrate that you're already doing your target job.

If you can do those new things without asking permission, just look for an opportunity and go for it. Of course you won't always be able to just start doing that new job, so you may need to think of other ways to get experience with your target job's duties. For example, maybe you're aiming for a promotion from Consultant to Senior Consultant, and the main difference between those two roles is that a Senior Consultant mentors other Consultants. Mentoring probably isn't something you can just do, so ask your manager if there are any good mentoring opportunities where you can be useful. "I'm really comfortable with the Consultant role, and am already documenting processes and creating training for new Consultants. If there are any Associate Consultants that need a mentor, I would love to work with them."

In the sections below, you'll build your case for a promotion, and the strongest component of your case will be that *you're already doing that job*. When you go to your manager to ask for a promotion using the method in this book, you will say something like, "I looked into it, and I think I've been doing the Senior Business Analyst job for the past few months. What else can I do to make things official with a promotion to Senior Business Analyst?"

I made a worksheet you can use to help define your roadmap and track your results as you make progress toward your goal. You can get it for free at <u>FearlessSalaryNegotiation.com/extras</u>.

3. Document your accomplishments and accolades

A big step toward making your case for a promotion is to document your results. Many people are uncomfortable with this step, and this is why they often find themselves waiting for a promotion to come to them instead of going after it. But it's up to you to make sure your accomplishments are recognized. Many managers are so busy that they may not be aware of what specific things you're doing to excel at your job. This is how you'll make sure your manager knows you are excelling at your job and ready for this promotion.

Accomplishments

Accomplishments are the things on your roadmap that you've done to demonstrate that you're ready for this promotion.

Once you've begun acquiring experience in line with your desired promotion, you should start documenting your accomplishments immediately. Just keep a spreadsheet or a text document where you jot things down as you do them.

Note that I said "jot things down". You're not writing a book about your accomplishments, you're keeping brief notes to use later when you build your case.

Record them in this format: Verb → noun → result.

"*Verb → noun*" is the thing you did. "*Result*" is the value added by the thing you did.

Here are some examples:

- Documented teammate onboarding process to make it reusable and to help decrease the time to productivity when new people join our team.
- Took online seasonal forecasting course to help with 2016 forecasting effort.
- Mentored Jeff as he built a client's blogging application in Ruby so that he can work on other Ruby projects in the future.

Note that this can be a useful format on your résumé as well. Most people just list the "Verb noun" part in their "Accomplishments" or "Experience" section, but they're missing an opportunity to describe the value they brought to the business by doing that thing. The "to result" part is how you communicate that value.

"I shoveled snow" isn't nearly as compelling as "I shoveled snow so that you can get your car out of the garage."

Having trouble thinking of things you've accomplished? Here are some questions to get your mental wheels turning:

- When did you go the extra mile for a client?
- How have you saved your team money?
- How have you made your team more efficient?
- What was your most recent learning experience?
- Have you made any suggestions that worked well and improved your team?

Accolades

Accolades are praise and awards you've received over the past several months. There's a good chance you already have accolades in your inbox if you know where to look. Start by searching your inbox for phrases like "thank you", "well done" and "great job" to see if you already have accolades from clients or coworkers. When you find good examples, move them over to a separate folder so that it's easy to find them again later. You can also use that folder to capture new accolades as they come in.

The two main types of accolades you're likely to find are specific praise from a client or coworker, and awards or recognition for a job well done. For specific praise from a client or coworker, record who gave the praise, and either a summary of their feedback or a specific quote from them if you have one. For awards and other forms of recognition, record the award name or description, and the project or accomplishment that earned you the award.

Here are a couple examples:

- ACME Corp—"Shannon really nailed this project. She kept us on track and informed the whole time, and did a great job of identifying risks well ahead of time. She made this project easy for us." —Tom Thompson, VP of HR
- Spotlight Award—For working three straight weekends on pre-sales for the ACME Corp deal to close it before end of year 2014.

While you're collecting examples of accolades, keep an eye out for accomplishments you forgot about. If you find any new accomplishments, make sure you go back and add them to your list of accomplishments.

4. Prepare your case

The best way to prepare your case is to write it down. As it turns out, you'll also want to have a written summary of why you deserve your promotion later on (see the "Present your case" section below), so we're going to kill two birds with one stone in this section by building an email that summarizes your case.

Here's what your case for a promotion will look like once you've written it down. I've numbered each section on the left side so we can talk about it afterward. You can also get this template at FearlessSalaryNegotiation.com/extras.

1	<u>To:</u> [Your manager's email address]
2	<u>Subject:</u> [Your name] promotion discussion—follow-up
3	Hi [Your manager's name]
4	Thanks for your time the other day. As I mentioned in our conversation, I would like to be considered for a promotion

	to **[target job title]**.
5	I've been working very hard to prepare for this opportunity, and I think I am ready. Here are some of my accomplishments over the past several months:
6	• **Verb noun to result** • **Verb noun to result** • **Verb noun to result** • **Verb noun to result**
7	And here is some feedback I've received from clients and co-workers over the past several months—their feedback speaks louder than anything I could say:
8	• **Client or co-worker name—"Quote" or general feedback documented in email or survey** • **Client or co-worker name—"Quote" or general feedback documented in email or survey** • **Client or co-worker name—"Quote" or general feedback documented in email or survey**
9	I believe the accomplishments and feedback above show that I am ready for this move, and for greater responsibility and compensation. I look forward to hearing what else you need from me to help make this happen.
10	Thanks again for your time and consideration! All the best **[Your name]**

Now, all you need to do is go through the template and replace anything in **bold** with the appropriate piece of information. This should be pretty easy because you've already done all the hard work. Feel free to edit this email to make it your own. This is just a template to get you started and show you the bare necessities you should include to make this as useful as possible.

Let's go section by section to build your email and make your case.

1. Address

You're writing this to your manager or whoever you will speak to about your promotion.

2. Subject

Make sure you include your name in the subject, and make it clear exactly what this email is about.

3. Greeting

Keep it short and sweet: "Hi Tina" will do. The bolded part is "Your manager's name" because I'm assuming you'll send this written request to your manager. If you're sending it to someone different, you'll want to change that to their name.

4. Introduction and request

Cut right to the chase and make it brief. Be as specific as possible about which job you're pursuing.

You'll note that the example refers to a conversation that has already happened ("Thanks for your time the other day."). That's because you won't send this email cold—it will be a follow-up to a verbal conversation if at all possible. We'll talk about that conversation more in the "Presenting your case" section below.

5. & 6. Accomplishments sections

Lay out your case as succinctly as possible. You should list no more than five accomplishments, so be sure to pick your strongest ones. This email isn't a complete historical record of everything you've ever done for the company. This is a skimmable document that makes a strong case for whoever is holding the purse strings to give you a promotion. You want the person reading this to think, "It looks like he's already doing this. Why haven't we already promoted him?"

One of the benefits of preparing your case ahead of time is that you can be confident that your case is strong before you present it. If you have trouble with this section, that's a red flag that your case may not be as strong as you anticipated, and you may not be ready to ask for this promotion. This isn't an ironclad rule, but I recommend covering a reasonable amount of time (several weeks or a few months) in this section so that your case is as compelling as possible when you present it.

7. & 8. Accolades sections

Again, this should be brief, but should highlight your best results from the past six months to a year. This isn't a complete record, it's a skimmable list that should raise eyebrows when others see it. Remember that the person approving a promotion may not know who you are, so you're giving them a short summary of your accolades to let them know that they should be impressed with you because other people are impressed with you.

This section is less crucial than the "Accomplishments" section, but it really helps. If you have trouble completing this part, you may still move forward with your request, or you may not. Some jobs are very solitary and simply don't garner accolades from clients or peers. I strongly recommend you have at least a couple items in this section before you present your case, but if your "Accomplishments" section makes a very strong case on its own, this section may not be necessary.

9. Conclusion and repeated request

State your request and make your case again as concisely as possible. No more than two or three sentences.

10. Signoff and signature

Thank your manager for her time and keep it brief.

Everything has now come together so that you know what you're pursuing, and you have a written case that summarizes why you should be promoted. This should help clarify your own objectives, and it will provide a handy reference for you as you present your case.

5. Present your case

Now you're ready to present your case and request your promotion. The proof is in the email you drafted. You have a list of things you've done that demonstrate that you're already doing your target job, and you have praise from clients and colleagues to really drive things home.

Although you've written a strong email that makes your case well, I don't recommend dropping that on your manager without some sort of warning. First, you should meet with your manager and ask for your promotion, then you'll follow up on your request by sending the email you composed.

Schedule a meeting to ask your manager for your promotion

If you have regular 1-on-1s with your manager, then you should bring this topic up in your next 1-on-1. If you don't have regular 1-on-1s scheduled, or if your 1-on-1 is frequently cancelled, you should reach out to your manager and let her know that you would like to meet soon to talk through some questions you have. Try to get a specific date and time on the calendar so that you can prepare for the conversation and so that you can be sure the conversation happens. You may need to take some initiative here to ensure that you have an opportunity to talk with your manager.

Once you're having this conversation, you can say something like, "I've been thinking about my career path, and I would like to talk with you about being promoted to Senior Business Analyst." Hopefully your manager will talk with you about this and give you some sense as to how likely a promotion might be. Because you have been working hard and have done your homework, you will already be prepared to back up your request with your accomplishments and accolades. You'll want to emphasize that you've already been working hard to demonstrate your readiness for this promotion, and let your manager know you'll follow up with a short, written summary of your request after your meeting.

Send your email after you've spoken to your manager

Once you've spoken to your manager, review the email you drafted in the "Prepare your case" section above, and make any changes that seem necessary after your conversation. You don't want to send outdated information in the email. Once you've made any updates, go ahead and send it along to your manager for review and consideration.

You might be wondering why you're sending an email that says the same thing you asked for in your meeting. The email acts as a record of your request, and it is forwardable—this is the key component. After you ask for your promotion, your manager will almost certainly have to run your request up the chain of command. At every stop along that chain, someone will need to be convinced that you've earned your promotion, approve it, and pass it on to the next link in the chain for approval. Your email makes your case clearly and succinctly and will make your manager's job easier, which increases the likelihood of your promotion being approved.

Once you've sent the email, the actual promotion is largely out of your hands. As we discussed earlier, there are many factors that companies consider when giving promotions, and some of those factors have nothing to do with you specifically. All you can do is make the most compelling case possible and hope that you get what you're asking for.

If you get what you asked for, congratulations! Your work here is done!

If you don't get your promotion, work with your manager to formulate a plan

If you didn't get what you asked for, you should ask your manager to help you formulate a plan to achieve your goal. "I'm disappointed that I couldn't be promoted to Senior Business Analyst. Can we please talk about what I need to do, specifically, to earn that promotion?"

Your manager may be able to work with you to put a plan and timeline in place so that you know specifically what you need to do to get your promotion. This is also a good outcome as it provides clarity and gives you a clear path to follow.

You may need to consider other options

Sometimes you won't get what you asked for, and your manager won't be able to offer a plan to achieve your goals. That's disappointing, but it's also an informative outcome: You now know that the promotion you feel you deserve isn't attainable at your current company or in your current part of that company.

The first thing you should do is take some time to do some soul searching. It's possible you're simply not as prepared to make that jump as you thought you were. Listen carefully to your manager's feedback and consider whether you jumped the gun. Sometimes, the surest way to a promotion is time and experience, and neither of those can be rushed.

After some soul searching, it may be time to start looking elsewhere for better opportunities where you can grow and be compensated as you feel you should be. You may be undervalued or *other*-valued in your current position at your current company.

What do I mean by "*other*-valued"? It's possible you're extremely good at what you do and that you have accomplished a lot in your current role, but that your specific company or industry simply doesn't value your skillset. Maybe you're really, really good at client-facing customer service, but your company is outsourcing that function to another company or is working to automate customer service as much as possible. Or maybe you're very strong in a certain technology that your company just doesn't use very much.

Either way—if you're undervalued or *other*-valued at your current company—it may be time to start searching elsewhere for better opportunities.

Looking ahead

Now that the potentially bad outcome is out of the way, let's talk about the good outcome you were pursuing and hopefully have achieved—you got your promotion! Now what?

By earning this promotion, you have demonstrated that you're already doing your new job at a level that merits that title. Start pursuing your next challenge by identifying the job you'll target next time you pursue a promotion. The sooner you start learning and demonstrating the necessarily skills for your next job, the sooner you can revisit this process and start preparing your case for your next promotion.

What about a raise?

Raises are such an important subject, I'm dedicating an entire chapter to them. In the next chapter, "How to negotiate your next raise", I'll walk you through the process of requesting a raise to bring your compensation in line with your market value.

Still, I would be remiss if I didn't at least give a general overview of the "raise" component of a promotion here. So this section is really just a description of what is likely to happen if you get promoted and don't focus on pay at all.

Standard raises

Most companies have some sort of policy in place to handle standard promotions and accompanying raises. Some companies simply have a policy that dictates a certain increase for each pay grade you move up. For example: If you move up one pay grade, you get a 4% raise; if you move up two pay grades, you get a 7% raise.

Some companies might do a more rigorous analysis by looking at your current pay, tenure with the company, time since your last promotion or raise, and other factors. At the end of this process, they'll pick some number—usually a percentage of your current salary—that represents the raise you'll get along with your promotion.

Very rarely, a company will promote you by changing your title and job responsibilities without increasing your pay. This might happen if you make a lateral move, which might mean you're pursuing a new job where you have little experience and will need to be trained. It might happen if the company is struggling financially and simply can't afford to give raises at the time of your promotion. It might happen because you specifically asked for a promotion, but did not specifically ask for a raise (this would be pretty unusual, but it's possible).

How to find out what your raise will be for this promotion

So how do you find out what your raise will be when you're promoted? Just ask when you're requesting your promotion. You're already requesting your promotion in two ways: first, you're scheduling a 1-on-1 with your manager to request your promotion; second, you're following up with a written request via email. Those are both great opportunities to ask about a raise as well.

You literally just need to add a single sentence to your conversation with your manager and to your follow-up email. During your conversation, I suggested you say something like this: "I've been thinking about my career path, and I would like to talk with you about being promoted to Senior Business Analyst." All you need to do is add one more sentence, "I'm also curious what sort of raise might accompany this promotion." In your follow-up email, just add that sentence to the end of the "introduction and request" section.

That's it! All you're doing is letting your manager know you want this promotion and making sure she knows that you anticipate an accompanying raise. That will give your manager an opportunity to let you know what the typical raise might look like or she might tell you that there's no raise available with the promotion you're pursuing.

If the available raise isn't enough, you may need to negotiate or consider other options

If the accompanying raise isn't sufficient, you may need to negotiate a bigger raise. I'll cover that process in more detail in "How to negotiate your next raise".

If there's no raise available with the promotion that you're pursuing, you may need to consider other options by either pursuing a different promotion or looking for opportunities outside of your current company.

Summary

A promotion is acknowledgement that you have taken on responsibilities that align with the next job in your career path. Requesting a promotion is simply requesting that your company acknowledge that you are already doing things that align with a different role by giving you the title and pay associated with that role.

The process to ask for a promotion has five steps:

1. Define your goal
2. Produce results to show you're ready
3. Document your accomplishments and accolades
4. Prepare your case
5. Present your case

1. Define your goal

There are two main types of promotion: straight-up and up-and-over. In either case, you need to determine *specifically* where you want to be. Determine which specific job you want to be promoted into.

Once you've determined the specific job you're targeting, learn enough about it that you can identify the differences in the requirements for that job and your current job. The differences between your current job and your target job are your roadmap— those are the things you need to gain experience with to demonstrate that you've earned this promotion.

Before you continue, take some time to evaluate your target job and ask yourself if you really want to do that job. Sometimes, learning more about a target job might help you realize that it's not a good fit for you.

2. Produce results to show you're ready

Managers don't generally give promotions and raises based on *potential*; they give promotions and raises based on *results*. Your task is to demonstrate that you're already doing the job you're asking for.

When you defined your goal, you created a roadmap of differences between your current job and target job—now it's time to follow that map to gain the experience you need to show you're ready for your promotion. Your plan is to do your target job, then ask to make it official with a promotion.

3. Document your accomplishments and accolades

As you acquire new skills and find ways to do the job you aspire to, be sure to record your accomplishments and accolades—they are the foundation of your case for your promotion.

4. Prepare your case

The best way to lay out your case is to write it down. You'll build an email to send to your manager to formally request your promotion later on, so you'll prepare your case by writing that email. Here's a brief summary of each section of your email.

Greeting—Keep it short and sweet.

Introduction and request—Cut right to the chase and make it brief. Be as specific as possible about which job you're pursuing. This is also where you should ask about an accompanying raise if you earn your promotion.

Accomplishments sections—Start with a short introduction explaining that these are the things you've accomplished that demonstrate your readiness for the new role or raise. Then list your accomplishments (no more than five) in a bulleted list.

Accolades sections—Start with a short introduction explaining that this is feedback you've gotten over the past several months. Then list your accolades (no more than five) in a bulleted list.

Conclusion and repeated request—State your request and make your case again as concisely as possible. No more than two or three sentences.

Signoff and signature—Thank your manager for her time and keep it brief.

Now you've got a short email that summarizes your case for the promotion you're pursuing, and you'll send this email after a verbal discussion with your manager.

5. Present your case

First, you want to verbally request your promotion from your manager. It's best if you can do this in a regular 1-on-1, or you might want to specifically schedule a short meeting to talk this over. Be persistent—it can sometimes be difficult to arrange this meeting if your manager is usually pretty busy.

When you verbally request the specific promotion that you're pursuing, be sure to emphasize that you're already doing the things that justify your request.

Once you've had the verbal discussion, you should review the email you composed in the "Prepare your case" section and make any updates that are needed after your conversation. Once you've updated the email and you're comfortable that it reflects your goals and makes the best possible case for your request, send it to your manager.

If you don't get your promotion, work with your manager to formulate a plan

Even if you've put in the work and presented an excellent case, you may not get the promotion you requested. If this is the case, you should ask your manager to help you formulate a plan to achieve your goal.

But sometimes a promotion at your current company just isn't in the cards. If that's the case, do some soul searching to determine if you just need to be patient and continue acquiring experience before you're ready to make that next move.

If you feel you've put in the work and demonstrated that you're ready for a promotion, but it still isn't available, you may be *other*-valued at your current company. In other words, you have a robust skillset and experience, but they simply aren't that valuable at your current company. In this case, you may need to look for opportunities at other companies that value your specific skillset and experience.

What about a raise?

Most companies have a standard raise amount for most promotions. You should ask your manager about your promotion's accompanying raise during your 1-on-1 where you request your promotion, and again in your follow-up email. If the standard raise is satisfactory, you probably don't need to do anything as it will almost always be included with your promotion. If the standard raise is unsatisfactory, you may need to negotiate for a bigger raise. See the "How to get your next raise" chapter for a detailed overview of this process.

CHAPTER 7

How to get your next raise

Hiring people is expensive and risky. Each new hire costs thousands of dollars. This is why companies are often open to "market adjustments"—by paying employees something close to market value, they keep experienced, proven employees at the company, save the expense of hiring a replacement, and avoid the risk of hiring a new person who is unproven.

This chapter is about getting a "big" raise of 8% or more—often described as a "market adjustment"—rather than a standard merit increase or a small "cost of living" increase.

As we discussed earlier in "Do you have to quit your job to get a big raise?", getting a big raise can sometimes be difficult without changing companies because raises are often predetermined and limited. But it *can* be done, and there's usually no harm in seeing how much of a raise you can get.

The raise process

Your manager, her manager, and someone in Finance look at salaries across the company and on your team, and they see lots of numbers. Your salary is one of those numbers, and it's mostly based on the value you add to the company. Maybe it was set when you were hired, or during your last merit increase, or when you were moved to a new department, but that number—your salary—was set in the past.

When there's a discrepancy between your current salary and the value of your skillset and experience at your company, there's an opportunity for you to get a raise. Sometimes management will rectify this discrepancy on its own, but most of the time you'll have to bring it to their attention by requesting a raise.

The process for getting a raise is similar to the process for getting a promotion—you define your goal, demonstrate that you've earned it, and then present your case. But there are differences between requesting promotions and requesting raises. Promotions are mostly *qualitative*, explicitly focused on title and responsibility, and only implicitly affecting your salary. Raises are mostly *quantitative*, explicitly focused on salary and implicitly focused on responsibility.

Justifying your raise request

Your primary justification for requesting a raise is that your value to the company has changed since your current salary was set, and that is good reason to reevaluate and adjust your salary to reflect your increased value to the company. This means that many of the reasons people might suggest to justify a raise aren't very effective. "I've been here for two years now" isn't a very compelling reason for a raise. Why? Because businesses mostly exist to make money, and they pay people higher salaries because those people help the companies make more money. You may still be adding exactly the same value to the company as you did when you were hired two years ago—in that case, there's no compelling business reason to pay you more money.

But while time in your job doesn't *explicitly* justify giving you a raise, it could *implicitly* help you make the case for a higher salary because you may have acquired new skills, taken on new responsibilities, or otherwise found new ways to add value to the company since you were hired. *Those* are compelling reasons to pay you more money.

Here are some examples of changes that might justify a salary increase:

- **Your qualifications have changed**—You have earned a certification, or a degree, or taken some training, or learned a new skill.
- **You have taken on more responsibility**—You are managing people or projects that you weren't when your current salary was set. Or maybe you're managing some part of the business that you weren't before.
- **The job market has changed**—There's been a shift in the market so that your skillset is in higher demand now than it was when you initially took your job.

In all three of these examples, there's a common theme: You are more valuable now than you were when your salary was last set. *That* is why you're asking for a raise.

Here's a high-level view of our process for requesting a raise:

1. Define your goal
2. Document your accomplishments and accolades
3. Prepare your case
4. Present your case

Let's walk through each step in more detail.

Before you get started, I recommend that you get the tools and templates I've made to help you work through the raise process. Get them for free at <u>FearlessSalaryNegotiation.com/extras</u>.

1. Define your goal

How do you define your goal when you're pursuing a raise? You estimate the market value for your skillset and experience and adjust that number to account for how valuable your skillset and experience are at your specific company.

Estimating the market value for your skillset and experience

Estimating your market value is so important to salary negotiations that this book includes an entire chapter dedicated to the topic. That chapter walks you through estimating your market value step-by-step. If you have not already read it, I strongly recommend you go back and read the chapter on "How to estimate your market value" before you continue.

Adjusting your market value estimation for your specific company

Once you've estimated your market value, you need to adjust that estimate to account for your value at your specific company. This is an important step because you're requesting a raise from your *company*, not from your *industry*, and the value of your skillset and experience to your company may not mirror the entire industry.

This is a very subjective adjustment. Below, I've listed some things you can consider when making this adjustment. For each one, think about whether it indicates that your skillset and experience are more or less valuable at your company than they are to the industry in general.

- How is the company performing lately? Do things seem to be going well, or have things been tight?
- Is your company hiring a lot of people to fill positions like yours? This may indicate the company has a strong need for your skillset and experience.
- Have there been layoffs lately?
- Have your peers been promoted or given large raises recently?

- Have bonuses been bigger or smaller lately?
- Has your manager recently given you either positive or negative feedback about your performance?

After considering all of these things and coming up with your own criteria, make a subjective judgment about whether you should adjust your market value up or down to account for your company's current situation. If you decide you *should* adjust your market value, estimate how much of an adjustment you should make. Chances are the value of your skillset and experience to your company is within about 10% of your market value either way, but it could be even more or less depending on your specific company and industry.

An example

Let's expand a bit on the example we used in "How to estimate your market value". In that example, Alison is a Project Manager making $65,000 a year in the Construction industry and she estimated her market value at $80,000, give or take. She also found that other project managers in her industry and region were making around $75,000, and she knows that a project manager who left her company earlier in the year was making $73,000.

Her market value is a good starting point for estimating the amount of the raise that she should request, but she also needs to calibrate her request to account for what she knows about the current situation at her company.

Alison has proven to be a good project manager for a few years at her company, so she's a known quantity who produces known results. Even if her company *did* find a good replacement for her, it would probably cost them about $80,000 and they would be hiring an unknown quantity with unproven results.

She has noticed that several other junior project managers have been hired in the past several months, and she's actually training one of them right now. This indicates that the company has a pretty high demand for project managers, and she's valuable because she's helping train new people. She has also noticed the company has been getting a lot of new projects recently, so it seems like sales have picked up and the company is doing well. This is supported by the fact that last year's bonuses were larger than they had been in previous years.

So it seems like the company is doing pretty well, and Alison is particularly valuable because new projects are coming in and she's helping train and educate the new project managers the company has hired.

Alison can reasonably request a raise to about $80,000 because that is her approximate market value and, although project managers in her industry and region are paid around $75,000, she's particularly valuable to her company. Her company also seems to be doing pretty well recently, so it's likely the growing business will value her skillset and experience more than other local companies might. This seems like a pretty big request, but the research she has done supports it.

You may already have everything you need to request a raise

Now that you've estimated your market value and have adjusted that estimate to account for your value at your specific company, you have your goal. Now it's time to move forward and make your best possible case to justify your goal.

Real talk: You may not need most of the remaining information in this chapter to get a nice raise. Your best ammo is the market mid-point data, augmented with a general sense of how you stack up against an "average" employee doing your job. So you could stop reading right now, call your manager up and say, "The mid-point for my job in our industry is $80,000 and I'm only making $65,000. Can we adjust my salary to align with the market?" Sometimes, that's all it takes. Some companies' HR departments are very attuned to the market, and expect they'll need to adjust salaries to align with the market over time. Your request could be just the push they need to look at your particular situation and make an adjustment.

The problem is you can't really know whether this sort of request will be sufficient until *after* you've made it. And since you don't know what you don't know, the best strategy is to present the most compelling case possible for your raise up front.

How do you do that?

2. Document your accomplishment and accolades

Before we dive in here, let me tell you that the rest of this chapter is going to look a *lot* like "How to get your next promotion". I really wrestled with whether I should present promotions and raises as a single concept in a single chapter. I decided there are subtle differences and that companies have different motivations for each thing. Those subtle differences were enough that I felt they should be separate chapters. So what you're reading isn't just a hasty copy-and-paste job. These processes—asking for a promotion, and asking for a raise—are different, but they're also similar.

Remember that your primary reason for requesting a raise is that the salary you're being paid doesn't reflect your current value to the company. That salary was set some time in the past, so your argument is that you are more valuable now than you were when your current salary was set.

So you need to identify the specific reasons—the things you've done since your current salary was set—why your value exceeds your salary. These are your *accomplishments*. You should also document positive feedback from your colleagues and clients, demonstrating that your work has positive impact on the company, and showing that others have noticed the additional value you bring to the company. These bits of positive feedback are your *accolades*.

Accomplishments

Accomplishments are things you've done to add additional value to your company by helping it make more money or save money.

As you become more experienced in your job, you'll usually see things you can do to make things more efficient. Sometimes your manager will ask you to do those things, and sometimes you'll find them on your own. The things you do to make your company more efficient are the things that add additional value to the company. I'm not talking about simply doing your job. I'm talking about doing things that demonstrate increased productivity in your job and add additional value to your company.

Let's look at our example of Alison, a Project Manager. What sort of accomplishments might demonstrate that she is making the company more money or saving the company money? If she was hired with an expectation that she would manage three big projects at a time, then she can make the company a lot more money if she manages four big projects at a time, and continues to manage them well. She could also save the company money by streamlining Project Management processes at her company. She could find tools to make her job and her peers' jobs easier, she could create a new process that eliminates some steps in each project, or she could create training that synchronizes all of the Project Managers so they're following a common process that makes auditing and bookkeeping easier for the Accounting team.

In short, Alison can add more value to the company by increasing her productivity and the productivity of her peers.

She can also add more value to the company by taking on responsibilities outside of her normal job description. One way she could do this is by taking some things off of her manager's plate, allowing her manager to do more productive things and gaining her some industry-specific experience in the process.

As you accomplish new things and find new ways to make or save your company money, keep a spreadsheet or a text document where you jot things down as you do them. Note that I said "jot things down". You're not writing a book about your accomplishments, you're keeping brief notes to use later when you build your case.

Record them in this format: *Verb → noun → result*.

"*Verb → noun*" is the thing you did. "*Result*" is the value added by the thing you did, preferably quantified in dollars.

Here are some examples:

- Actively managed four concurrent projects (up from three), bringing an additional $20,000 in revenue this year.
- Created a better Sales handoff process in order to make the process faster and to avoid common misunderstandings that often cost time and money during projects. Made the company an additional $5,000 on one project by identifying an undersold project during this process.
- Took control of the new project assignment process from Tiffany, saving her about two hours a week.

Note that this can be a useful format on your résumé as well. Most people just list the "verb → noun" part in their "Accomplishments" or "Experience" section, but they're missing an opportunity to describe the value they brought to the business by doing that thing. The "result" part is how you communicate that value.

"I shoveled snow" isn't nearly as compelling as "I shoveled snow so you can get your car out of the garage, saving you 30 minutes."

Having trouble thinking of things you've accomplished? Here are some questions to get your mental wheels turning:

- What things are you doing more of than you did when your current salary was set?
- How have you made yourself and your peers more productive so that they can do more work with the same resources?
- What new responsibilities have you taken on that you didn't have when your current salary was set?
- What other ways are you making your company more money or saving money?

Accolades

Accolades are praise and awards you've received over the past several months. Accolades are helpful because they demonstrate to your company's management that others have noticed the great job you're doing, even if your managers haven't.

There's a good chance you already have accolades in your inbox if you know where to look. Start by searching your inbox for phrases like "thank you", "well done" and "great job" to see if you already have accolades from clients or coworkers. When you find good examples, move them over to a separate folder so it's easy to find them again later. You can also use that folder to capture new accolades as they come in.

The two main types of accolades you're likely to find are specific praise from a client or coworker, and awards or recognition for a job well done. For specific praise from a client or coworker, record who gave the praise, and either a summary of their feedback or a specific quote from them if you have one. For awards and other forms of recognition, record the award name or description and the project or accomplishment that earned you the award.

If possible, you should focus on accolades that have a quantitative component (additional money made or money saved), but this isn't strictly necessary.

Here are a few examples:

- ACME Corp—"Alison really nailed this project. She kept us on track and informed the whole time, and did a great job of identifying risks well ahead of time. She made this project easy for us and even helped us finish three weeks ahead of schedule." —Tom Thompson, VP of HR
- Spotlight Award—For working three straight weekends on pre-sales for the ACME Corp deal to close it before end of year, bringing in an additional $15,000 in revenue for 2014.
- "Alison introduced a new time tracking tool that saves every Project Manager about three hours a week in administrative time. This has saved our team over a hundred hours so far this year."—Christina Smith, PMO Director

While you're collecting examples of accolades, keep an eye out for accomplishments you forgot about. If you find any new accomplishments, make sure you go back and add them to your list of accomplishments.

3. Prepare your case

The best way to prepare your case is to write it down. As it turns out, you'll also want to have a written summary of why you deserve your raise later on (see the "Present your case" section below), so we're going to kill two birds with one stone in this section by building an email that summarizes your case.

Here's what your case for a raise will look like once you've written it down. I've numbered each section on the left side so we can talk about it afterward. You can also find this example at FearlessSalaryNegotiation.com/extras.

1	**To:** [Your manager's email address]
2	**Subject:** [Your name] salary adjustment discussion—follow-up
3	Hi **[Your manager's name]**
4	Thanks for your time the other day. As we discussed, it has been **[amount of time]** since **["my last significant salary adjustment" OR "since I was hired"]**, and I would like to revisit my salary now that I'm contributing much more to the company. I've been researching salaries for **[job title]** in **[industry]** industry, and it looks like the mid-point is around **[mid-point from your research]**. So I would like to request a raise to **[target salary]**.
5	I've been working very hard to find ways to contribute value to our company. Here are some of my accomplishments over the past several months:
6	• **Verb noun to result** • **Verb noun to result** • **Verb noun to result** • **Verb noun to result**
7	And here is some feedback I've received from clients and co-workers over the past several months—their feedback speaks louder than anything I could say:
8	• **Client or co-worker name—"Quote" or general feedback documented in email or survey** • **Client or co-worker name—"Quote" or general feedback documented in email or survey**

	• **Client or co-worker name—"Quote" or general feedback documented in email or survey**
9	I believe these accomplishments and feedback show that my work merits a higher salary, and **[target salary]** seems well aligned to the current market and with the additional value I am adding to our company since my current salary was set. I look forward to hearing what I can do to help make this happen.
10	Thanks again for your time and consideration! All the best **[Your name]**

Now, all you need to do is go through the template and replace anything in **bold** with the appropriate piece of information. This should be pretty easy because you've already done all the hard work when you did your research earlier. Feel free to edit this email to make it your own. This is just a template to get you started and show you the bare necessities you should include to make this as useful as possible.

Let's go section by section to build your email and make your case.

1. Address

You're writing this to your manager or whoever who you'll speak to about your raise.

2. Subject

Make sure you include your name in the subject, and make it clear exactly what this email is about.

3. Greeting

Keep it short and sweet: "Hi Tina" will do. The bolded part is "Your manager's name" because I'm assuming you'll send this written request to your manager. If you're sending it to someone different, you'll want to change that to their name.

4. Introduction and request

Cut right to the chase and make it brief, specifically listing your desired salary.

Notice that I recommend you state the midpoint from your market research *before* your desired salary. This is so that the first number is a market number—a fact that is determined by external forces—and that should soften up your manager for your request. Your request will seem much more reasonable when presented immediately after the market-set midpoint.

You may also notice that the example refers to a conversation that has already happened ("Thanks for your time the other day."). That's because you won't send this email cold—it will be a follow-up to a verbal conversation if at all possible. We'll talk about that conversation more in the "Presenting your case" section below.

5. & 6. Accomplishments sections

Lay out your case as succinctly as possible. You should list no more than five accomplishments, so be sure to pick your strongest ones. This email isn't a complete historical record of everything you've ever done for the company. This is a skimmable document that makes a strong case for whoever is holding the purse strings to give you a raise. You want the person reading this to think, "She's already adding so much more value to the company then when she was hired. This seems like a totally reasonable request given all the money she has made and saved us since then."

One of the benefits of preparing your case ahead of time is that you can be confident that your case is strong before you present it. If you have trouble with this section, that's a red flag that your case may not be as strong as you anticipated, and you may not have earned as much of a raise as you thought. This isn't an ironclad rule, but I recommend covering a reasonable amount of time (several weeks or a few months) in this section so that your case is as compelling as possible when you finally present it.

7. & 8. Accolades sections

Again, this should be brief, but should highlight your best results from the past six months to a year. This isn't a complete record, it's a skimmable list that should raise eyebrows when others see it. Remember that the person approving this raise may not know who you are, so you're giving them a short summary of your accolades to let them know that they should be impressed with you because other people are impressed with you.

This section is less crucial than the "Accomplishments" section, but it really helps. If you have trouble completing this part, you may still move forward with your request, or you may not. Some jobs are very solitary and simply don't garner accolades from clients or peers. I strongly recommend you have at least a couple items in this section before your present your case, but if your "Accomplishments" section makes a very strong case on its own, this section may not be necessary.

9. Conclusion and repeated request

State your request and make your case again as concisely as possible. No more than two or three sentences.

10. Signoff and signature

Thank your manager for her time and keep it brief.

Everything has now come together so that you know what you're pursuing, and you have a written case that summarizes why you should be given a raise. This should help clarify your own objectives, and it will provide a handy reference for you as you present your case.

4. Present your case

Now you're ready to present your case and request your raise. The proof is in the email you drafted. You have a list of things you've done that demonstrate that you're adding more value than you were when your current salary was set, and you have praise from clients and colleagues to help drive things home.

Although you've written a strong email that makes your case well, I don't recommend dropping that on your manager without some sort of warning. First, you should meet with your manager and ask for your raise, then you'll follow up on your request by sending the email you composed.

Schedule a meeting to ask your manager for your raise

If you have regular 1-on-1s with your manager, then you should bring this topic up in your next 1-on-1. If you don't have regular 1-on-1s scheduled, or if your 1-on-1 is frequently cancelled, you should reach out to your manager and let her know that you would like to meet soon to talk through some questions you have. Try to get a specific date and time on the calendar so that you can prepare for the conversation and so that you can be sure the conversation happens. You may need to take some initiative here to ensure that you have an opportunity to talk with your manager.

Once you're having this conversation, you can say something like, "I've been doing some research, and I think I might be pretty far below the midpoint for my job in the current market," or "I've been here for three years now and have gotten pretty small raises along the way despite taking on more and more responsibility. I've looked into the market value for my current job and it seems like my pay is a bit below the midpoint. I wonder if we can talk about what it would take for me to get a raise to bring me closer to the market pay for my job."

Hopefully your manager will talk with you about this and give you some sense of how likely a raise might be. Because you have been working hard and have done your homework, you will already be prepared to back up your request with your research, accomplishments and accolades. You'll want to emphasize that you've already been working hard to find ways to make yourself and your peers more efficient and productive, and that you think you've already justified the salary you're requesting. Then let your manager know you'll follow up with a short, written summary of your request after your meeting.

Send your email after you've spoken to your manager

Once you've spoken to your manager, review the email you drafted in the "Prepare your case" section above, and make any changes that seem necessary after your conversation. You don't want to send outdated information in the email. Once you've made any updates, go ahead and send it along to your manager for review and consideration.

You might be wondering why you're sending an email that says the same thing you asked for in your meeting. The email acts as a record of your request, and it is forwardable—this is the key component. After you request your raise, your manager will almost certainly have to run your request up the chain of command. At every stop along that chain, someone will need to be convinced that you've earned this raise, approve it, and pass it on to the next link in the chain for approval. Your email makes your case clearly and succinctly and will make your manager's job easier, which increases the likelihood of your request being approved.

Once you've sent the email, the actual raise is largely out of your hands. As we discussed earlier, there are many factors that companies consider when setting salaries, and some of those factors have nothing to do with you specifically. All you can do is make the most compelling case possible and hope that you get what you're asking for.

If you get what you asked for, congratulations! Your work here is done!

If you don't get your raise, work with your manager to formulate a plan

If you didn't get what you asked for, you should ask your manager to help you formulate a plan to achieve your goal. "I'm disappointed that we couldn't adjust my salary to $75,000. Can we please talk about what I need to do, specifically, to earn that raise? And can we talk about a timetable for when it might be feasible?"

Your manager may be able to work with you to put a plan and timeline in place so that you know exactly what you can do to earn your raise. This is also a good outcome as it provides clarity and gives you a clear path to follow.

You may need to consider other options

Sometimes you won't get what you asked for, and your manager won't be able to offer a plan to achieve your goals. That's disappointing, but it's also an informative outcome: You now know that the salary you feel you deserve isn't attainable at your current company or in your current job.

If your request for a salary increase isn't granted, and your manager can't help you formulate a plan to earn it, you should take some time to do some soul searching. It's possible you're simply not as prepared to request the salary as you thought you were. Listen carefully to your manager's feedback and consider whether you jumped the gun. You may have overestimated the value of certain projects or skills at your particular company.

After some soul searching, it may be time to start looking elsewhere for better opportunities where you can grow and be compensated as you feel you should be. You may be undervalued or *other*-valued in your current position at your current company.

What do I mean by "*other*-valued"? It's possible you're extremely good at what you do and you have accomplished a lot in your current role, but your specific company or industry simply doesn't value your skillset. Maybe you're really, really good at client-facing customer service, but your company is outsourcing that function to another company or working to automate customer service as much as possible. Or maybe you're very strong in a certain technology that your company just doesn't use very much.

Either way—if you're undervalued or *other*-valued at your current job—it may be time to start searching elsewhere for better opportunities.

What about a promotion?

It's also possible you should *actually* be requesting a promotion because the salary you requested is above the top of your current paygrade (see the "How companies manage their salary structures" chapter for more information on paygrades). Your manager may tell you this explicitly—"That raise would put you above the top of your paygrade"—or implicitly—"That would move you higher than most of your peers." Either of these responses may mean that your best opportunity to keep things moving forward may be to pursue a promotion.

This can also happen when the market data you found doesn't distinguish between levels of a position (Project Manager I, Project Manager II, etc.) in the same way as your company. Your research may indicate the midpoint for your job in your industry is $50,000, but maybe your company has split that job into two tiers—Junior and Senior. Moving up to $50,000 may move you above the top of the "Junior" paygrade, while it would leave you below the midpoint for the "Senior" paygrade. You may need to pursue a promotion to move yourself into a higher paygrade so that you have more room to increase your salary closer to the market midpoint.

If you find that you really should be pursuing a promotion, you're in luck! The previous chapter, "How to get your next promotion", will guide you through the process.

Looking ahead

Now that the potentially bad outcome is out of the way, let's talk about the good outcome you were pursuing and hopefully achieved—you got your raise! Now what?

By earning this raise, you have demonstrated that you're helping your company make more money or save money beyond what was expected of you last time your salary was set. But don't sit still! Now is a good time to start looking ahead at your career path, identifying positions where you can move to a higher paygrade, giving yourself more room for your next raise.

Summary

Raises are different than promotions because raises focus on the *quantitative* value that you add to the company whereas promotions often focus on *qualitative* measurements and accomplishments.

The process to ask for a raise has four steps:

1. Define your goal
2. Document your accomplishments and accolades
3. Prepare your case
4. Present your case

1. Define your goal

To define your target salary, estimate the market value for your skillset and experience and adjust that estimate to reflect your current value to your company. Start by reading "How to estimate your market value", then adjust your market value estimate to reflect the current situation at your specific company. Your value to your company is probably within 10% or so of your market value.

Once you've done this analysis, you have your goal—your target salary.

2. Document your accomplishments and accolades

Your primary reason for requesting a raise is that your current salary doesn't reflect your value to the company. So you need to identify the specific reasons—the things you've done since your current salary was set—why your value exceeds your salary. Try to list accolades that clearly demonstrate that you either made the company more money or saved the company money in some way. These accomplishments and accolades are the foundation of your case for your raise.

3. Prepare your case

The best way to lay out your case is to write it down. You'll build an email to send to your manager to formally request your raise later on, so you'll prepare your case by writing that email. Here's a brief summary of each section of your email.

Greeting—Keep it short and sweet.

Introduction and request—Cut right to the chase and make it brief. Start by stating the market midpoint you found in your research, then ask for your target salary.

Accomplishments sections—Start with a short introduction explaining that these are the things you've accomplished that demonstrate the additional value you bring to the company since your last major salary adjustment. Try to focus on accomplishments that have a numeric (preferably dollars) component. Then list your accomplishments (no more than five) in a bulleted list.

Accolades sections—Start with a short introduction explaining that this is feedback you've gotten over the past several months. Then list your accolades (no more than five) in a bulleted list. Try to focus on accolades that show where you've either made the company money or saved money.

Conclusion and repeated request—State your request and make your case again as concisely as possible. No more than two or three sentences.

Signoff and signature—Thank your manager for her time and keep it brief.

Now you've got a short email that summarizes your case for the raise you're requesting, and you'll send this email after a verbal discussion with your manager.

4. Present your case

First, you want to verbally request your raise from your manager. It's best if you can do this in a regular 1-on-1, or you might want to specifically schedule a short meeting to talk this over. Be persistent—it can sometimes be difficult to arrange this meeting if your manager is usually pretty busy.

When you verbally request your target salary, be sure to emphasize the ways in which you are adding greater value to the company in your role. Focus on ways you have increased efficiency or productivity, and ways in which you've made or saved the company money.

Once you've had the verbal discussion, you should review the email you composed in the "Prepare your case" section and make any updates that may be needed after your conversation. Once you've updated the email and you're comfortable that it reflects your goal and makes the best possible case for your request, send it to your manager.

If you don't get your raise, work with your manager to formulate a plan

Even if you've put in the work and presented an excellent case, you may not get the raise you requested. If this is the case, you should ask your manager to help you formulate a plan to achieve your goal.

But sometimes your company simply can't or won't be able to pay you the salary you feel you deserve. If that's the case, do some soul searching to determine if you just need to be patient and continue acquiring experience before you're ready to command the salary you're targeting.

If you feel you're adding more value than when your salary was set, and you can quantify the money you're making or saving for the company, you may be *other*-valued at your current company. That's my way of saying that you have a robust skillset and experience, but your particular skillset and experience simply aren't that valuable at your current company or in your current industry. In this case, you may need to look for opportunities at other companies that value your specific skillset and experience.

What about a promotion?

You may find that you are unable to reach your target salary because your current paygrade tops out below your target salary. In that case, you may need to pursue a promotion to a job with a higher paygrade so that you have more room for your salary to increase. See the "How to get your next promotion" chapter for a detailed overview of this process.

Thanks for reading, and a special offer

Thanks for reading *Fearless Salary Negotiation*! You can help other people find the book and get paid what they're worth when you **leave some feedback on Amazon.** Just search for "Fearless Salary Negotiation" and you'll see this book listed.

Fearless Salary Negotiation is one component of a full suite of tools and resources to help you get paid what you're worth. The suite includes the book, case studies, video courses, and other great resources.

A special offer: Learn more about the full suite of tools and resources available for *Fearless Salary Negotiation* at FearlessSalaryNegotiation.com, and *use the offer code* **paperback1** *to get $5 off when you upgrade.*

There are also free tools, templates, and other extras available at FearlessSalaryNegotiation.com/extras. And you can join my newsletter to receive discounts on future products and get my best content on career management and salary negotiation delivered for free directly to your inbox.

- Josh

PS Let's stay in touch! Here's where you can find me online:

Email: josh@joshdoody.com
Twitter: @JoshDoody
LinkedIn: linkedin.com/in/joshdoody
Blog: JoshDoody.com

55538268R00106

Made in the USA
Lexington, KY
26 September 2016